Best Tea Shop Walks in Leicestershire & Rutland

Paul & Sandra Biggs

Published by Sigma Leisure – an imprint of Sigma Press, 1 South Oak Lane, Wilmslow, Cheshire SK9 6AR, England.

British Library Cataloguing in Publication Data
A CIP record for this book is available from the British Library.
ISBN: 1-85058-603-9

Typesetting and Design by: Sigma Press, Wilmslow, Cheshire.

Cover: Manor Farm Tea Room, Barton in the Beans *(Sandy Biggs)*
Maps: Alan Bradley
Photographs: the authors

Printed by: MFP Design & Print

Disclaimer: the information in this book is given in good faith and is believed to be correct at the time of publication. No responsibility is accepted by either the author or publisher for errors or omissions, or for any loss or injury howsoever caused. Only you can judge your own fitness, competence and experience.

Preface

Our first thought on Tea Shop Walks in Leicestershire and Rutland was, 'Are there any?' With over 20 years of walking experience in the area, we thought we knew just about everything the region had to offer. Surprise, surprise, careful research revealed that yes, there are many tea shops tucked away off the beaten track, and the array of cream teas available is quite outstanding.

Tea shops come in all shapes and sizes and are found in the most unusual places. By far the most popular in Leicestershire and Rutland are located within farmhouses or garden centres. However, in our unquenchable thirst for a pot of tea or coffee together with a home-made scone and strawberry jam at the end of a walk, we discovered tea rooms hidden away at a windmill, stables, antique shop, craft shop, steam railway station waiting room and a 17th- century hall, as well as the more traditional tea shop in a secluded village or market town.

Having found the right tea shops it was not too difficult to put together a selection of 28 good circular walks as Leicestershire and Rutland share a well-marked network of footpaths and bridleways. The walks vary in length between two and eight miles, and should satisfy the needs of most walkers. Why not sample one of our shorter walks as an afternoon's stroll or spend a day on a longer walk, tasting an area that is steeped in history or local culture. The beautiful countryside in Leicestershire and Rutland is certainly one of contrasts.

Now a short word on unification. From 1st April 1997, Rutland regained its county status, which had been lost since 1974. The old boundaries of Rutland have been restored with no changes taking place to existing county lines. Unification was also granted to the city of Leicester. Although the city is still run by Leicester City Council, officialdom decrees that the city of Leicester is legally known as the City and County of Leicester. The remaining part of old Leicestershire has become new Leicestershire.

Whether your preference for walking is in the rocky outcrops of Charnwood Forest, the lovely hills of High Leicestershire or through the chocolate-box villages of Rutland, we have ensured that this book of walks covers the rich and varied landscape that is relatively unknown to tourists and visitors from outside of the area. There are many hidden delights to discover, whilst historically Leicestershire and Rutland have a wealth of treasures buried away from the prying eyes of motorists who charge through Leicestershire on the M1. Here's a real chance to get to know this beautiful part of Middle England better, while at the same time enjoying an early morning coffee, lunch or a cream tea from a tea shop that you probably didn't even know existed. Watch those bathroom scales though!

Lastly, a word of thanks to Graham Beech, Sigma Press for enccouraging us to write this book. We also wish to thank our young sons, Daniel and Tommy, who seem to be growing up very quickly, for their company on the shorter walks. Also, Trudie Colotto for her help in looking after the boys when we were researching the longer walks. Thanks also to Sarah Greenhalgh for once again deciphering our writing and typing the manuscript on the word processor. But above all, thanks to you for purchasing the book. We do hope that you enjoy the walks as much as we did.

Paul and Sandy Biggs

Contents

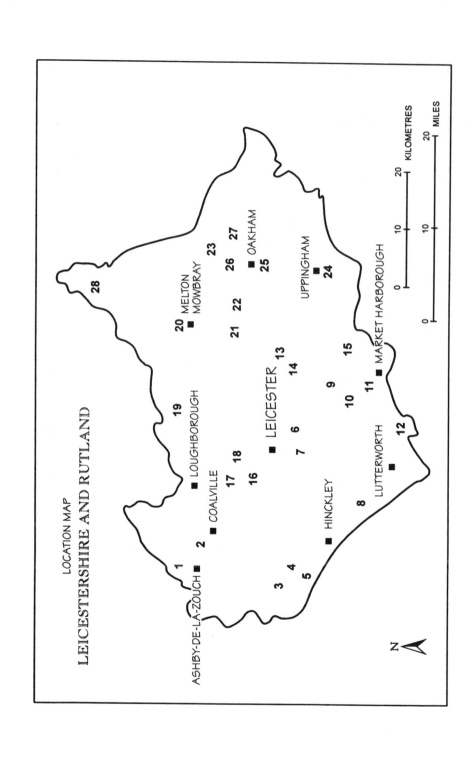

LOCATION MAP
LEICESTERSHIRE AND RUTLAND

Introduction

Leicestershire and Rutland is an area of diverse landscape, rich in rolling green uplands, low valleys, woods, rivers and canals, with many beautiful villages dotted about the districts. There is a sharp divide between east and west, with the natural dividing line being the River Soar and Soar Valley. In the west lie the rocky outcrops of Charnwood Forest, while to the east are the rolling hills of 'High Leicestershire'. Probably the most spectacular scenery of Leicestershire and Rutland is found in the Charnwood Forest region. There you will find volcanic ash formation from 700 million years ago when volcanoes erupted and deposited ash over the western half of the area, forming some of the oldest rocks in Britain.

To many people, this Heart of the Shires region instantly conveys a picture of hunting. It is true that Leicestershire and Rutland are home to some of the most famous packs in England. The best known is The Quorn, which has hunted in the north since the late 17th century. The other packs associated with the region are The Femie that meets in the south, The Pytchley which is a predominantly North-amptonshire pack, sometimes meeting in the extreme south, The Atherstone over in the west, The Belvoir to the north-east and The Cottesmore in Rutland. If you do see the hunt in full stride it is a colourful sight and whatever your views are on fox hunting, it is part of Leicestershire and Rutland's tradition.

Many changes have taken place in recent years but none more so than to North West Leicestershire. An area of industrial past (much of the Leicestershire coalfield stretches below the surface) is now being transformed as the National Forest planting scheme takes place. At Moira, which is the headquarters for the National Forest, a new visitors' centre has been built on the former coal mine. Anyone with an interest in industrial archaeology will want to visit the Moira Blast Furnace Museum. Here also, a grant has been awarded from the National Lottery Fund for a visitors' centre next to the museum. At the end of 1996 it was announced that the Ashby Canal, which prematurely ends at Snarestone, will be dug out again to Measham and re-opened to pleasure traffic. A new marina and wharf at

Measham will bring tourism and prosperity once again to this derelict site.

The Lie of the Land

East Leicestershire is referred to as 'High Leicestershire' since much
of it is on an iron and marl stone plateau between 500 feet (152.5m)
and 600 feet (183m) above sea level. This forms part of the Stone
Belt, which crosses England from Dorset to the Yorkshire coast. The
focal point of the area is Burrough Hill, at 690 feet (210m) one of the
highest hills in East Leicestershire. This Iron Age hill fort commands
extensive views and from the toposcope you can see Leicester and
Charnwood Forest to the west, Billesdon Coplow to the south and far
into Rutland in the east.

The valley of the River Wreake and River Eye runs east to west
through the borough of Melton, where villages such as Asfordby,
Frisby, Hoby and Rearsby date back to Danish foundation. At Melton Mowbray the River Wreake flows into the town, but emerges out
as the River Eye. Quite curious! The local countryside around Melton rivals that of the Cotswolds with green rolling hills, lush valleys,
unspoilt villages and old churches built in yellow ironstone.

West Leicestershire has arguably the finest countryside in the
county, especially in the Charnwood Forest area. This honeypot is
roughly seven miles by four miles, and is located to the south of
Loughborough. Although the ancient forest no longer exists, the
granite rocky outcrops where some of Britain's oldest rocks are to be
found certainly do. The highest point in Leicestershire is at Bardon
Hill, 912 feet (278m) and although widespread quarrying has taken
place to the hill it is still very much in evidence. Nearby is Beacon
Hill, a Bronze Age settlement, where a number of early Bronze Age
implements have been unearthed. Below the rocky outcrop of the
summit are 73 hectares (180 acres) of woodland, bracken-covered
slopes and rhododendron bushes.

Probably the best known part of Charnwood Forest is Bradgate
Park. This is Leicestershire's largest and most popular country park,
extending to 344 hectares (850 acres). The country park includes
Bradgate Park, which is an ancient hunting and deer park, and
Swithland Wood, noted for its rich collection of plants, moths, but-
terflies and birds. This area of parkland is a mixture of heath,

bracken, grass-covered slopes, rocky outcrops and small woodlands where herds of red and fallow deer roam free, especially in and around the valley of the River Lin.

Leicestershire's main river, the River Soar, flows through the borough of Charnwood on its way to the River Trent. The combined river and canal system meanders through the Soar Valley, where pretty waterside villages stand either side of the waterway. Charnwood has an abundance of footpaths that allow access to the diverse scenery in this district. Whether it be over the rolling green hills, through scattered woods, along the banks of the Soar or across open countryside, you will not be disappointed.

The borough of Hinckley and Bosworth covers 105 square miles of rolling countryside in South West Leicestershire. Much of the area is predominantly mixed farmland, extending from the wide plains in the south-west to the undulating land in the east. Woodland plays an active part in the topography with some rocky knolls and granite outcrops evident near Markfield. The largest woods are at Burbage Common which extends some 89 hectares (220 acres), and has recently become a country park with a visitors' centre. Bosworth Park remains largely intact with several beautiful woodland walks available. Currently the Ashby-de-la-Zouch Canal winds its way through south-west Leicestershire to its present terminus just north of Snarestone. Having the look of a river in places, this canal is part of a 2000 mile system of canals and rivers administered by British Waterways. The northern reaches of the Ashby Canal are currently the subject of a major restoration project as mentioned earlier.

North Leicestershire falls into two main categories. North West Leicestershire, or Ivanhoe Country as it is more often called, is now at the heart of the National Forest. The region is relatively flat and ideal for mixed farming. Much of the landscape has been changed over the years due to opencast mining around Ibstock and Ashby-de-La-Zouch. The Leicestershire coalfields in the Coalville area are now redundant, and since the closure of Whitwick Colliery in 1986 great effort has been put into redeveloping the old mines into greenfield sites.

One of the great landmarks of the area is Breedon Hill. The hill was inhabited in the Iron Age and is encircled with earthworks dating from the first century BC. Breedon on the Hill village is dominated by the hill, which is made up of carbon limestone and towers nearly 200 feet (61m) above the surrounding countryside. Standing on top of the summit is a 13th-century Norman church, which makes an excellent viewpoint to study North West Leicestershire.

Over to the north-east is the broad sweep of the Vale of Belvoir, overlooked by a steep clay and limestone scarp that terminates by Belvoir Castle. A string of pretty villages stretch along this narrow strip of North East Leicestershire, from Bottesford and Muston in the north down to Hose, via Harby, Plungar, Barkestone and Redmile, in the west. All of these villages are linked together by the Grantham Canal, opened in 1797. Although abandoned in 1936, the canal still retains a certain amount of water. It is hoped that one day the canal will be re-opened by the restoration society who are currently working extremely hard to restore it back to its former glory.

South Leicestershire is made up of three districts: Harborough, the largest, Blaby, and Oadby and Wigston. Harborough extends for 230 square miles, encompassing all the ingredients of a peaceful, pastoral scene with open rolling hills, meadows and green fields. Stretching from the border with Warwickshire in the west to Rutland in the east, it borders Northamptonshire to the south and Leicester to the north.

The Leicester line of the Grand Union Canal flows right through South Leicestershire into the City of Leicester. At Foxton there is a magnificent staircase of ten locks built in 1814. By the side of the locks is the site of the Foxton Inclined Plane, a truly fine piece of Victorian engineering. At the basin below the Market Harborough arm of the Grand Union Canal, the Leicester Line joins, which gives the district a total of 25 miles of peaceful, meandering waterways. Croft Hill is the most substantial hill in Blaby district and in the area, standing at 400 feet (122m). The hill is the cause of some controversy today. The quarry owners of the hill have discouraged the rights of villagers and walkers to the hill. A local group has been formed to preserve rights to use the hill for recreational purposes and to try to stop the quarry company from blasting away the remaining half. No compromise has yet been reached.

Rutland is only about 15 miles long and 15 miles wide. The west of the county is structured around a marl stone escarpment which rises to 700 feet (213m) in places. To the east, Rutland also forms part of the oolitic limestone Stone Belt, also evident in East Leicestershire. Sandwiched in between is Rutland Water. The small county is bounded by Leicestershire to the west and north, Lincoln-shire to the east and Northamptonshire to the south. Oakham is the county town to the north-west, while the only other town, Upping-ham is found in the south-west. There are, however, more than 40 villages and hamlets. The Welland is the main river in Rutland and runs along the southern boundary with Northamptonshire. This river is one of the main sources for Rutland Water.

Rutland Water had a huge impact on the area when it was con-structed in the 1970s. The reservoir spans 1255 hectares (3100 acres) with a storage capacity of 124 000 million litres (27 million gallons). It was built to satisfy the rising demand for water at that time from the developing towns of Northampton, Peterborough, Corby, Milton Keynes, Daventry and Wellinborough. Not only does it provide water for domestic and industrial consumption, but also offers tremendous recreational amenities. Water is pumped into the reservoir at Tinwell from the River Welland and at Wansford from the River Nene, being sent through 12 miles of pipes and tunnels. The dam is constructed mainly from upper lias clay obtained from the land which was subsequently flooded. The crest of the dam is 4000 feet (1219m) long and 133 feet (40.5m) above the lowest sec-tion of the base, which is 2900 feet (884m) in cross section. The res-ervoir's depth is 110 feet (33.5m).

The Walks

These 28 routes, all circular, enable the walker to explore outstand-ing unspoilt countryside, which is not accessible to the motorist, at leisure. The length of the walks varies between two and eight miles, with the majority of the routes falling in the four to five mile cate-gory. Parents with young children or those who prefer an afternoon's stroll will find the shorter walks ideal, especially secure in the knowledge that there is a welcoming cup of tea or coffee and a choice of home-made cakes to suit all tastes available at the end of the walk. For the more ambitious, the longer walks attack the challenging rug-ged landscape of East and West Leicestershire. The views from all of these walks should be enjoyed – all too soon the day's walking will be over and it will be just a distant memory until, of course, the next time.

The Tea Shops

Everyone enjoys a cuppa – it is, in fact, Britain's most popular pastime, drinking tea. There is surely no better way to complete a country walk than having a cream tea and a pot of tea or coffee. The tea shops or tea rooms have been included in this guide book on their own merits. All have unique pleasures of their own, one is housed at a windmill currently under restoration, another re-lives the early days of the flying machine, while a third has probably the finest collection of colourful teapots in Leicestershire and Rutland on show. Obviously the locations of the tea shops have had a bearing on the locations of the walks. You will not be disappointed, we would say that had it not been for the tea shops we may never have found such interesting, remote places around which to devise our walks. One point to always bear in mind is that establishments are subject to change. So before setting off on your walk, we strongly recommend that you telephone the tea room to be sure of your refreshment. It would be a complete disaster should the establishment be closed on your intended visit due to an unexpected emergency.

Tea rooms are usually kept to the highest of standards with cleanliness next to godliness. Some have luxuriously fitted carpets, please respect this by ensuring that you remove muddy boots before entering. Bon appétit!

Public Transport

There is an extremely good network of bus and train services covering Leicestershire and Rutland, with all main towns and some larger villages having both bus and railway connections. All of the walks can be reached by public transport, and full details are given in the fact file at the beginning of each walk. On the rare occasion where no bus or train service exists to coincide with the starting point, we have given alternative suggestions as to where to start the walk. Since deregulation of bus companies, the number of private bus operators has increased dramatically and services run to all points in the area. It is strongly recommended that all times and services are checked beforehand by telephoning Busline. This telephone service is sponsored by Leicestershire County Council through the bus operators and the information is provided by the Public Transport Unit, County Hall, Glenfield, Leicester. They will post you a bus timetable, free of charge, for the area that you intend to visit – providing they have the timetable in stock. For all enquiries please telephone Busline 0116 251 1411.

The privatisation of railways has also brought about a number of changes to railway lines and services within the counties. Midland Mainline Ltd operate the London St Pancras, Derby/Sheffield service that calls at Market Harborough, Leicester and Loughborough. Central Trains Ltd or Regional Railways are responsible for services that pass through Hinckley, Leicester, Melton Mowbray and Oakham. They also take charge of the Ivanhoe Line, with services calling at the intermediary stations of Barrow upon Soar, Sileby and Syston between Loughborough and Leicester. Again, we strongly recommend that you check availability of the service by telephoning the National Rail Enquiries at Derby. They are sponsored by all of the different railway operating companies to give impartial advice on national rail services. For all enquiries, 24 hours a day, please telephone 0345 484950 (charged at local rate).

Walking for Pleasure

Country walking is now one of the most popular outdoor pursuits in Britain. It is an extremely healthy pursuit even on the coldest of days, provided that you wrap up well. A walk in the countryside clears the mind of day-to-day problems, allowing you to unwind. The batteries are recharged, giving you a more positive outlook on life.

A good pair of walking boots are essential for the longer walks, while a strong pair of shoes with a thick sole may be sufficient for the shorter walks. Trainers, high heels or sandals are definitely not suitable as they offer little or no support in the ever changing countryside. If purchasing a pair of walking boots for the first time, consult a reputable outdoor shop. The specialist there will give advice on types and styles of walking boots, even assisting with the fitting. Make sure that you try the boots on over a pair of walking socks. The shop will supply you with a pair of walking socks as they hope to sell the boots and socks to you! We always find it advisable to wear a pair of ordinary socks with a pair of walking socks on top to help the boots feel comfortable and to keep your feet warm on cold days.

As the good old British weather is so changeable, a cagoule and over-trousers must be carried in a rucksack at all times. Jeans must never be worn as they restrict your walking rhythm, and in wet weather become heavy and cold thus reducing body temperature. Always wear an extra pullover or a fleece. It is simple to remove any surplus clothing if the going gets warm and to put those discarded items into your rucksack. It is a problem if you do not have adequate clothing with you, particularly if the temperature drops a number of degrees when walking on high ground. In winter always go prepared for the unexpected. Cover up your head with a woolly hat which can be pulled down over the ears. Wear a pair of gloves to keep your hands warm right from the word go.

In late 1996 Ordnance Survey brought out a new series of Explorer maps for various areas of Great Britain, replacing selective maps in the Pathfinder series. Rutland and parts of the surrounding area are covered under OS Explorer 15 Rutland Water and Stamford. All of the walks featured in this book have details of the relevant Ordnance Survey Landranger and Ordnance Survey Pathfinder maps that should be taken with you. We have given clear, concise instructions for the route of each walk but it is a good idea to carry the maps with you, either in the rucksack or in a plastic map case.

Make sure you have a first aid kit in case of cuts or minor accidents. Always tell a neighbour or a friend of your intended walk and when you expect to return. Ensure that they realise that you have returned home – you don't want them telephoning the police or rescue services with a false alarm. If you have a mobile telephone take this with you in the event of a dire emergency.

Food is a matter of personal choice. Do always take a flask of hot tea, coffee of soup. Chocolate bars should be included for emergency rations. However, do not consume too much food – or you may not feel up to a cream tea at the end of the walk!

Tourist Information Centres

Ashby de la Zouch: North Street, Ashby de la Zouch, LE65 1HU Telephone 01530 411767

Bosworth Battlefield: Visitor Centre, Sutton Cheney, Market Bosworth, CV13 OAD Telephone 01455 292239. Open Easter to October.

Coalville: Snibston Discovery Park, Ashby Road, Coalville, LE67 3LN Telephone 01530 813608

Hinckley: Library, Lancaster Road, Hinckley, LE10 OAT. Telephone 01455 635106

Leicester: 7-9 Every Street, Town Hall Square, Leicester LE1 6AG. Telephone 0116 265 0555

Leicester: St Margaret's Bus Station, Leicester, LE11 3EB. Telephone 0116 251 1301

Loughborough: Town Hall, Market Place, Loughborough. Telephone 01509 218113

Market Harborough: Pen Lloyd Library, Adam and Eve Street, Market Harborough LE16 7AG. Telephone 01858 821270

Melton Mowbray: Melton Carnegie Museum, Thorpe End, Melton Mowbray, LE13 1RB. Telephone 01664 480992

Oakham: Flore's House, 34 High Street, Oakham, Rutland, LE15 6AL. Telephone 01572 724329

Rutland Water: Sykes Lane, Empingham, Oakham, Rutland, LE15 8PX. Telephone 01780 460321. Closed January/February.

Walk 1. Staunton Harold

Route: Staunton Harold Hall car park – Callan's Lane – Heath End – Dimminsdale Wood – The Ridgeway Path – Staunton Harold Hall – Staunton Harold Tea Room.

Start: Staunton Harold Hall car park (at the rear of the garden centre). GR 377218

Distance: 2¾ miles

Maps: OS Landranger 128 Derby and Burton upon Trent area, OS Pathfinder 852 Burton upon Trent.

Terrain: Estate paths, well waymarked. Excellent woodland path through Dimminsdale Wood. No steep climbs but plenty of wooded hills around.

Public Transport: None

By Car: Staunton Harold Hall is about four miles north-east of Ashby de la Zouch and signposted off the A453. Take the B587 towards Melbourne, then turn left for the main car park as directed. There is plenty of car parking at the rear of the hall, garden centre and Ferrers' centre.

The Tea Shop

Staunton Stables Tea Room is located in the Ferrers' Centre at the rear of Staunton Harold Hall. The original tea room there was established in 1984 and can seat 36, with room for a further 36 patrons outside in the magnificent courtyard. The proprietors, Michael and Alison Kemp, run a thriving business but always have time to greet visitors with a friendly, warm welcome.

Home-made cakes, pastries and lunches are served on lovely, rose-patterned china. The Staunton lunches consist of daily 'hot specials' such as beef cobbler or fruity lamb casserole, traditional oven-baked potatoes with various fillings, soup, toasted sandwiches and hot puddings. Afternoon and cream teas are served. On a sunny afternoon, why not eat 'al fresco' after the walk? Whilst enjoying your refreshments, do admire the unusual collection of ornamental tea pots and model cars that are displayed on the walls inside the tea room.

Pickles, preserves, Twinnings' teas and home-made cakes are available to take away at reasonable prices. Last hot food orders are at 16.45 (16.15 in the winter) and parties can be catered for by prior arrangement. This is a tea room that you can return to time and time again and not be disappointed with the service or menu.
Opening Hours: 10.30 to 17.00 (summer), 10.30 to 16.30 (winter). Closed on Mondays, except for bank holidays. Telephone 01332 864617

The Ferrers' Centre for Arts and Crafts

The craft centre is contained within the splendid Georgian stable block in the grounds of Staunton Harold Hall. The craftspeople are highly skilled and are proud of their reputation for excellence. Most of the workshops are open to the public daily from 11.00 to 17.00 (except Mondays) with the range of arts and crafts quite staggering. Do call in at the Victorian Model Workshop to view and perhaps purchase hand-made, one-off, mechanical and musical Victorian-style automata, clocks, models and caricatures of all kinds of people.

Staunton Harold Hall

The present house was built from 1763 by Washington Shirley, 5th Earl Ferrers, but includes part of two earlier houses. Staunton Harold dates back to Saxon times, when Harold was a Saxon owner. However, William the Conqueror gave the estate to Henry de Ferraris (later Earl Ferrers). The manor came to the Shirleys by marriage in 1423. Charles II then made Sir Robert Shirley a baron, and Queen Anne restored the earldom. In the 18th century, Lawrence Shirley, 4th Earl Ferrers, deliberately murdered his steward at the hall. The reason seems unclear, but what is certain is that the culprit was hung at Tyburn in 1760, despite his plea of insanity. In 1954 the Ferrers sold the estate, but the hall was later saved from demolition by Group Captain Leonard Cheshire VC in 1955, and converted into a home for the chronically sick. When he moved to new premises at Netherseal in 1985 the hall was purchased by the Ryder – Cheshire Mission. It is now a Sue Ryder home, exhibition centre, a volunteer training and research centre, Sue Ryder shop and coffee room. The grounds of the hall are open to the public all year round but not the hall.

Staunton Harold Church

The church is one of the few churches to be built during the Commonwealth. Although its looks give an impression of the 15th century, the actual date was 1653. It was erected by Sir Robert Shirley, an ardent royalist. Inside it is much as it was built, with 17th-century cushions and hangings, a wrought iron screen by Robert Bakewell, panelling and painted ceilings. There are monuments to the Shirley family. Upon entering the church, do read the inscription over the door. Now owned by The National Trust, the church is open 1st April – end of September, Saturday to Wednesday and bank holiday Mondays 13.00 – 17.00 (or sunset). October – Saturday and Sunday only. Admission is free, but donations are appreciated.

The Route

Walk to the top of the car park and where the road turns uphill, turn left at a yellow-topped waymarker post. Cross the field as shown by the arrow to the next waymark post and stile. Follow alongside Rough Heath Wood to reach the next stile. Climb and continue to the end of the wood, where another wooden stile is located.

Keep close to a hedge to come to an old stile by a metal gate. Pass to the right of the old stables to find a stile on to Callan's Lane. Turn right, passing the beautiful house at Heath End Farm then an even older farmhouse at Ley Farm. On the right is the car park for the Saracen's Head. Carry along the lane to the road junction. Turn right on to the road and walk to the turning to Staunton Harold, about 200 metres on.

Turn right on to the driveway and walk ahead for a further 200 metres to a yellow-topped waymark post. Join a grassy track which leads to a stile at the edge of Dimminsdale Wood. Follow the obvious woodland path through the wood, which is a reserve belonging to the Leicestershire and Rutland Trust for Nature Conservation. Do take care as the path overlooks disused and overgrown limestone quarries. At a 'V'-shaped stile inside the wood, turn right and follow the high level path uphill then round to the left. Climb six steps then follow around to the right to descend six steps. A walkway takes you uphill in the wood. Next continue on the rugged woodland path, enjoying some fine views of glorious countryside.

Pass a wooden post with the number 6 carved on the side and

Staunton Harold Hall and church, from across the lake

drop down a flight of steps towards a water-filled quarry called the Laundry Pool. The path meanders through the wood passing further numbered marker posts, which are fairly close together. Cross two wooden, one-hand footbridges in quick succession then turn right, climbing another flight of steps to reach an information board. From here stand and look at the old kilns where limestone was burnt for the production of lime. The Laundry Pool, now to your left, was quarried by the Earls Ferrers and 11 more lime kilns are now submerged on the quarry floor.

Continue ahead, climbing more steps to a wooden walkway. Cross a one-hand footbridge to reach a second information board at the road. Turn right along the road, passing the southern tip of the large Staunton Harold Reservoir. Turn right into the Severn Trent Reservoir car park then climb the steps ahead to follow the path that snakes uphill to a yellow-topped waymark post at a junction of routes. Now turn right on to the Staunton Ridgeway permissive path, opened on 28th September 1994 thanks to generosity of John Blunt, owner of the Staunton Harold Estates.

As you climb slowly there is a fine view of Staunton Harold church and hall. Pass through a stile, noting that all the stiles along the permissive path contain a quotation from Hilaire Belloc, on to a field-edge path. Follow alongside a wall, where the views are even better, then pass through a squeezer type stile to a track. In 50 metres turn right, and follow along a woodland path going downhill, quite steeply in one place. At the end of the wood, climb a stile, turn right on to an obvious path, then left along a grassy track. Turn right on to the Estate road to pass through the golden gates topped by the Ferrers' talbot and stag. Pass between the two lakes then follow signs for the Ferrers' Centre and Nurseries. Go round the rear of the hall to reach the entrance to the centre and Staunton Stables tea room. To complete the walk, turn left at the garden centre to reach the car park.

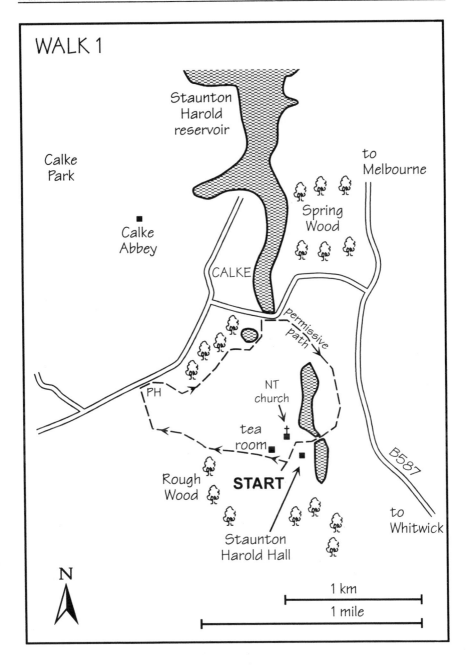

WALK 1

Staunton
Harold
reservoir

Calke
Park

to
Melbourne

Calke
Abbey

Spring
Wood

CALKE

permissive
path

NT
church

tea
room

Rough
Wood

START

Staunton
Harold Hall

PH

B587

to
Whitwick

N

| 1 km |
| 1 mile |

Walk 2. Ravenstone

Route: Beesley's Garden Centre – Ravenstone – Donington le Heath – Snibston – Ravenstone – Gardener's Rest Tea Room.

Start: Beesley's Garden Centre and Nurseries, Heather Lane, Ravenstone. GR 403135

Distance: 3 miles

Maps: OS Landranger 129 Nottingham and Loughborough area and OS Pathfinder 874 Loughborough (South).

Terrain: Well-used field paths and tracks. Small amount of road walking. No steep climbs.

Public Transport: Regular Coalville to Ravenstone and Ashby de la Zouch – Swannington – Ravenstone services are operated by Midland Fox.

By Car: Ravenstone is situated on the A447, two miles from the centre of Coalville. It can also be approached by the A50 Ashby de la Zouch – Markfield road. Parking is available at the garden centre for walkers, provided there is sufficient room. Otherwise park where you safely can in Ravenstone village.

The Tea Shop

The Gardener's Rest Tea Room is located in Beesley's Garden Centre and Nurseries on Heather Lane, Ravenstone. The small tea room was opened in 1991 and the current proprietor, Emma Hewitt, has been there since 1994. The glass conservatory is a real suntrap, as is the outside patio – although here the canopy offers welcome shade on hot days.

Emma runs a very friendly tea room with many regulars, especially at lunch time, dropping in from work. Hot snacks include jacket potatoes with an assortment of fillings, toasties and home-made soup. Cakes are Emma's speciality – you should try her raspberry pavlova or chocolate fudge cake – scrumptious.

Opening Hours: 10.00 – 16.30 Monday to Saturday, closed Wednesday. Sundays 10.00 – 13.00. Telephone 01530 832101.

Beesley's Garden Centre and Nurseries

It was in 1963 that this family business opened. The garden centre arrived first to be followed by the nurseries. Since then Beesley's has grown and grown, covering today 2.63 hectares (6½ acres) in total. If you want to know anything about plants these are the people to see. The garden centre sells fresh cut flowers, mainly grown locally, plants of all description and ornamental pots, as well as the more traditional products associated with the business. A personal service is given with specialist advice freely available.

Ravenstone

The village is famous for being the home of the railway engineer George Stephenson. His work in railway and mining is still very much connected with this area. Ravenstone's name is derived from the Anglo-Saxon Raunstone. The 'Raun' refers to the red rock strata of the area, while 'ton' means town. This name is mentioned in the Domesday Book. The parish church of St Michael and All Angels dates back to the early 14th century, and the land around the church has been declared a conservation area. One of the few cruck cottages left in Britain is found on Main Street, while Alton Grange where George Stephenson lived is found nearby.

The Manor House, Donington Le Heath

The Manor House is situated one mile south of the centre of Coalville, between the villages of Donington and Hugglescote. It is one of the oldest houses in Britain, dating to 1290. The house has a fascinating history, having been lived in by the lords of the manor and later by the tenant farmers. However, in the 1950s the house lay derelict and was used as a pig shed. Leicestershire County Council stepped in and completely restored the house between 1966 and 1973. Today it is virtually the same as it was in the days of its earliest owners. The Manor House is open from the Wednesday before Easter to 30th September (inclusive), Wednesdays to Sundays 14.00 – 18.00. Admission is free. Telephone 01530 831259.

The Manor House, Donington le Heath, dates from 1290

Coalville

Pleasantly situated on the edge of Charnwood Forest, Coalville is still a relatively young town, having grown out of the Industrial Revolution. Over a period of 170 years the town has evolved from a scattering of about 200 inhabitants along a rough track known as Long Lane to a thriving community of over 30 000 people.

Coalville's development was closely linked to the development of the coal mining industry and the arrival of the railway line. In 1833 the Leicester and Swannington Railway opened, engineered by Robert Stephenson, son of George Stephenson, connecting a number of coal mines in Long Lane and Swannington to Leicester. From here onwards Coalville grew rapidly, with the opening of more coal mines such as Snibston Number One and Number Two and Whitwick Colliery.

In 1986, Coalville's long association with coal mining came to an end when Whitwick Colliery closed. However, the rich heritage has not been lost thanks to the development of Snibston Discovery Park on the site of Snibston Number Two Colliery. This award-winning tourist attraction gives visitors the opportunity to explore a unique mixture of science, nature, history and technology. In the exhibition hall everyone will enjoy the hands-on experiments, there are over 30 of them, as well as the transport gallery. Outside you may join ex-miners in a lively surface colliery tour which will fascinate all the family. Open daily except Christmas Day and Boxing Day 10.00 – 18.00 (17.00 November-March). Telephone 01530 510851 or 813256.

The Route

From the car park at Beesley's Garden Centre and Nurseries, walk along the driveway to Heather Lane. Turn left on to the path adjacent to the road and follow it for 100 metres to a public footpath signpost. Climb the tall, wooden stile and an obvious path leads across the grassy field to another stile. A very short field path now cuts diagonally away to a stream.

Cross the footbridge then turn right, following alongside the stream. Go diagonally over the next field, which may be ploughed, and in this case follow round the field to the right, making for a white house where a public footpath signpost will be located. Rejoin the main route and turn right on to the grassy verge of the busy A447, heading in the Hinckley direction. Continue by the road for half a mile until finding a public footpath signpost opposite Kelham Bridge Farm.

Walk ahead into the field then follow the hedge around to the left to a concrete footbridge. Cross the stream to join a path that goes uphill passing alongside the water treatment works. A short section of enclosed path between hedge and railings soon opens out into a grassy field. From here there are interesting views of the surrounding landscape. Some are most pleasing to the eye, while others are in stark contrast with the opencast mining of the Ibstock area seen on the horizon. As you make your way ahead, do take care as there are **quite large holes just off the path** that have been left from the old sewer system.

Just before the electricity transmission lines, follow the field path around to the right then to the left before passing beneath the national grid lines. Go through a large hedge gap then walk ahead alongside the hedge. A short farm track then brings you to Berryhill

Lane. Continue along the lane for 250 metres, to a public footpath signpost. If you wish to visit the Manor House at Donington le Heath, carry on along the lane to the famous old building.

To continue the walk, turn left at this signpost, on to a field perimeter path following close to a hedge. Over to the right is Bardon Hill, the highest point in Leicestershire. Climb a wooden stile and turn left as indicated by the waymarker arrow. At the next yellow-topped waymarker post, continue alongside a hedge to reach a wooden stile by an old, metal farm gate. Walk along the field edge, which is rutted in places, going downhill to a large, metal gate. A farm track now takes you past the large farm buildings at Grange Farm and after passing through another farm gate, the tiny hamlet of Snibston is reached. Do stop and look at the tiny church of St Mary which dates back to 1150.

At the road, turn left and follow for a quarter of a mile to the junction with the A447. Cross to Jenny's Lane opposite to walk back into Ravenstone village. Upon reaching Leicester Road, turn left, passing The Plough, to come to Heather Lane. Turn left and it is but a short walk back to the garden centre and a delicious tea at the Gardener's Rest.

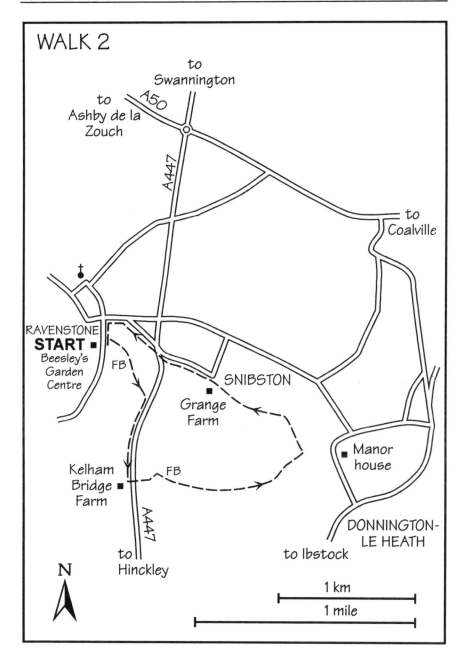

Walk 3. Shackerstone

Route: Shackerstone Church – Odstone Hall – Barton in the Beans – Carlton – Shackerstone Station – Shackerstone Church.
Start: St Peter's church, Shackerstone. GR 375066
Distance: 5 miles
Maps: OS Landranger 140 Leicester and Coventry area, OS Pathfinder 893 Tamworth.
Terrain: Mainly along well-defined field footpaths and bridleways. Flat, open countryside with extremely pleasant views. No climbs.
Public Transport: Very poor bus service to Shackerstone. Thursdays only from Shenton to Coalville, operated by TRS coaches. Saturdays only from Nuneaton to Ibstock, operated by Woods.
By Car: Shackerstone is situated midway between Hinckley and Ashby-de-la-Zouch. It is signposted from both the A447 and A444. Follow the B585 Market Bosworth road through Congerstone to reach the village. Limited street car parking by the church and Rising Sun public house.

The Tea Shops

On this walk there is a choice of two tea shops.

The Parlour Tea Rooms on Shackerstone Station have been open since September 1996. Prior to this they were known as The Victorian Tea Rooms. The tea room is the former station master's office in the station building which has been refurbished and re-decorated with the change of tenants. There is much railway memorabilia in the tea room and the buildings on the station platforms.

Joanne Richardson of M and W Catering runs a busy tea room which caters for railway personnel, visitors to the Battlefield line and casual callers, all of whom have different tastes in food. Hot food, roast dinners, sandwiches and rolls are available, along with the traditional fare of scones and jam. If the weather turns cold there is a large open fire in the centre of the tea room that gives off nearly as much heat as the steam trains in the station.

Opening Hours: 09.30 – 17.30 Saturdays, Sundays and bank holiday Mondays. (12.00 – 15.00 January to March.) Also, when trains are running, Wednesdays and Fridays during the summer. Please telephone beforehand for timetable of railway services. Telephone 01827 892842 (M and W Catering) or 01827 880754 (Shackerstone Station).

Manor Farm Tea Room in Barton-in-the-Beans has been run by Betty Jackson and her husband since 1987. Betty has become a cult figure in Leicestershire tea room circles, with patrons coming from far and wide to enjoy the warm welcome given to all. It is not hard to see why – all the delicious food that you eat is home-made, including the jam which oozes out from the scones. Eggs are free-range from their own hens which are kept on the farm. There is a super choice of food to enjoy in the cosy tea room or , in the summer, in the pretty garden. Do try Betty's Leicestershire Curd Tart – it is a 'must'.

Such is the popularity of the tea room you may have to wait a little while for a table. Cycling clubs from all over the county regularly call as do ramblers on organised walks. Nothing is too much trouble as Betty's aim is to please everyone who calls. If you are waiting for a table, spend some time looking round at the farm memorabilia. The lovely, restored red post box in the conservatory makes a fine starting point for the tour. Betty is fascinated by post boxes!

Opening Hours: 11.00 – 17.00 Wednesdays, Thursdays, Saturdays, Sundays and bank holiday Mondays in the summer. 11.00 – 17.00 Saturdays only in the winter. Telephone 01455 290362.

Shackerstone

This village is a popular destination for walkers as five different footpaths converge. The Ashby Canal also passes through the village and makes a colourful sight in summer with narrow boats moored by the towpath. Apart from the perpendicular tower, St Peter's church was rebuilt by the Victorians and is worth a visit.

The Battlefield Line starts at Shackerstone Station, and runs four and three-quarter miles to Shenton Station, next to Bosworth Battlefield. This preserved railway line is operated and maintained by volunteers from the Shackerstone Railway Society. The station building dates from 1873 and has been lovingly restored by the members and friends of the society. A museum has a magnificent collection of local railway relics, with many dating from the last century. Steam and diesel hauled trains operate from March to November and for details of fares and timetable, telephone 01827 880754.

The Church of St Peter, Shackerstone, dominates the village

The Route

From the church in Shackerstone, pass the Rising Sun public house to reach a T-junction of roads. Turn right and in 100 metres cross over the road bridge of the Ashby Canal where a junction of Leicestershire Round public footpath signposts is located. Bear left along the farm access track, quickly passing beneath the bridge of the Battlefield Line. 300 metres ahead a yellow-topped waymarker post indicates that the Leicestershire Round footpath goes over a field diagonally right.

Go over a one-handrail footbridge and make for a yellow-topped waymarker post in the far right-hand corner of the next field. Go through the large, ageing, metal gate on to a track. Turn right and follow the track around, going uphill. There are good views of the south-west Leicestershire countryside to enjoy as you make your way along this track for the next three-quarters of a mile.

At a myriad of public footpath signposts by Odstone Hall, turn right on to a vague but recognisable field footpath. After 400 metres climb a footbridge over a stream, then walk along a field perimeter

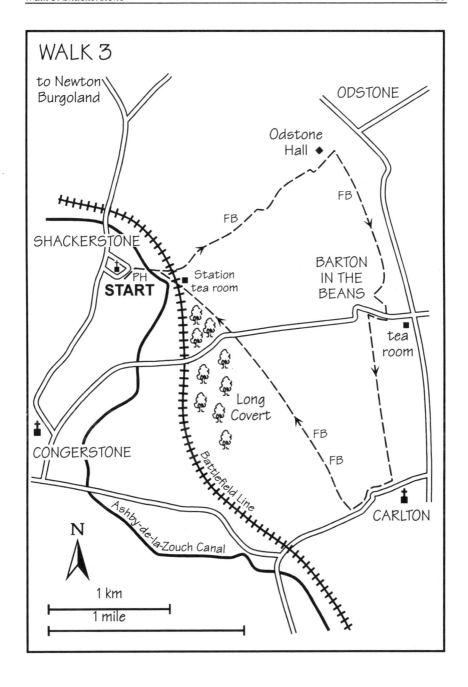

WALK 3

to Newton Burgoland

ODSTONE

Odstone Hall ◆

FB

SHACKERSTONE

PH
START

Station
tea room

FB

BARTON
IN THE
BEANS

tea
room

Long
Covert

FB

FB

CONGERSTONE

Battlefield Line

CARLTON

N

Ashby-de-la-Zouch Canal

1 km

1 mile

path next to a hedge. Numerous stiles are climbed on this obvious path that passes alongside many horse paddocks. In summer there is not much room between the hedge on one side and the electric fence on the other.

As Barton-in-the-Beans village approaches you need to turn left over a stile at the end of the horse paddocks on to a field perimeter path for 150 metres, still making towards the village. Climb a stile which is well hidden in the hedge to reach a path which leads you towards a house. The path then takes you past a white up-and-over door of a garage and into the village of Barton-in-the-Beans.

Turn right to pass the Baptist chapel, rebuilt in 1841. Walk through the village until reaching a public footpath signpost for Carlton. Go through two green gates in quick succession to a field path. Climb a stile each side of a dike then go slightly left to a gate. After two fields turn right on to a track for 50 metres, then turn left to rejoin the field path. Cross a number of fields on an obvious path, following the waymarker posts ahead to Carlton village.

Turn right along the road opposite St Andrew's church and walk along Main Street then Congerstone Lane to a public footpath signpost just past Carlton Grange. The field path passes alongside the house to a grey, metal gate. Continue ahead to a track, turn right, then go left over a stile. The field path now accompanies a hedge. After crossing a wooden footbridge, continue to a gate.

The path is extremely obvious. After striding over another footbridge, continue on in the same manner, following the Leicestershire Round signs on the yellow-topped waymarker posts. Cross the road by the north-east tip of a wood called Long Covert to rejoin the field footpath at Keeper's Cottage.

Make for Orange Hill Plantation, then climb a stile by the tip of the wood and skirt around the wood, going downhill to the footbridge over the railway at Shackerstone Station. The footbridge brings you on to platform one, where a side gate will be open if the station is closed. However, if the station is open you will have to walk through the booking hall, which is adjacent to the Parlour Tea Rooms. Turn right on to the access road, which now takes you alongside the tranquil Ashby Canal to the road bridge which was crossed at the start of the walk.

Retrace your steps along the road, turning left into the main part of Shackerstone village to return to the church.

```
┌─────────────────────────────────────────────────────────┐
│                                                           │
│            Walk 4. Market Bosworth                        │
│                                                           │
└─────────────────────────────────────────────────────────┘
```

Route: Market Bosworth – Sutton Lane – Bosworth Road – The Almshouse – Sutton Cheney – Bosworth Park – Market Bosworth.

Start: The War Memorial, Market Square, Market Bosworth. GR 406031

Distance: 4½ miles

Maps: OS Landranger 140 Leicester and Coventry area, OS Pathfinder 894 Leicester (West) and Market Bosworth.

Terrain: Easy walking along a gated road. Good footpaths over fields with a pretty woodland stroll through Bosworth Park.

Public Transport: A fairly frequent service from Leicester to Market Bosworth operated by Midland Fox. No Sunday service. A Thursday only Shenton to Coalville service run by TRS Coaches.

By Car: Use either the A447 Ashby to Hinckley road or A444 Nuneaton to Burton upon Trent road, then take the B585 to Market Bosworth. Parking is available in the cobbled market place.

The Tea Shops

On this walk there is a choice of two tea shops.

The Almshouse tea room at Sutton Cheney is found in the original stable block of the 17th-century almshouses. They were used for charitable purposes for over 350 years, but by 1976 had fallen into disrepair. Phil and Cherry Orton, the current owners of the tea rooms and restaurant, acquired the premises in 1984 and have lovingly restored The Almshouse as closely as possible to its original character.

Afternoon tea can be taken on the terrace overlooking the garden or inside the restaurant. The menu has a wide selection of sandwiches, salads, hot snacks and puddings to choose from, while all the lovely cakes are home-made. Full lunches or bar meals are also available, as is a traditional, home-cooked Sunday lunch. However, this is popular, so an early booking may be necessary. Phil, Cherry and staff are most obliging, so have no fear if you just fancy a cup of tea on the terrace – they will be happy to serve you this. But while you are there you should try the cream tea – it is delicious.

Opening Hours: 10.00 – 17.15, seven days a week. Telephone 01455 291050

Bosworth Tearooms are found along Shenton Lane, 400 metres from the centre of Market Bosworth. The tea rooms are handily placed to catch passing trade from visitors on the road to the battle-field. Opened in 1993, Jean and Tony Harkin have thrown open part of their lovely house to cater for the many cyclists and visitors to the area. The house was a former farmhouse, built over 100 years ago, with a long, gravelled front drive and well-kept garden.

Jean and Tony prepare and bake all the home-made cakes and scones at the house. They serve a number of different light snacks on toast, ploughman's lunches and sandwiches, but nothing fried. In the summer teas can be enjoyed in the conservatory or outside on the shaded drive.

Opening Hours: 10.30 – 18.00 Saturdays, Sundays and bank holiday Mondays. Weekdays – no set time. Try the door and see. Telephone 01455 290144

Market Bosworth

An attractive little market town which is probably the smallest in Leicestershire, being only slightly larger than many of the neighbouring villages. There are many fine Georgian buildings grouped around the cobbled market square, where on Wednesdays a retail market is held. In fact, a royal charter granted Market Bosworth the right to hold a market from 1285.

The town is just two miles from the battlefield so you do need to choose carefully when to visit. Throughout the summer special events take place on Bosworth Field, mainly on Sundays, so be warned. The town is famous for its flower festivals and displays, having won the final of Britain in Bloom. St Peter's Church supports a fine tower and spire visible from many miles around. Built in the 14th century, it contains a monument to Reverend John Dixie who died in 1719.

Market Bosworth Country Park

Owned by Leicestershire County Council, this 35 hectare (87 acres)

Sampling a cup of tea at The Almshouse tea room, Sutton Cheney

park is situated opposite Bosworth Hall Hotel along the B585. Once an ancient deer park, it is mainly a mature parkland with a lake and an arboretum with oaks and maples. There is a very pleasant walk that takes you through the arboretum into Bosworth Park. Although Bosworth Park is private, it contains a public footpath which is followed on this walk and is extremely pretty, especially in spring and autumn.

Sutton Cheney

A plaque commemorating the death of Richard III can be seen in St James's Church, which is next to the almshouse. It was here that Richard took his last communion on the eve of the historic Battle of Bosworth which took place on 22nd August 1485. The church dates to the 14th century, with a very large, squat tower. Inside is the tomb of the almshouse's original founder, Sir William Roberts. He was a local knight renowned for his good deeds. In 1612 he commissioned the building of six small almshouses for the poor men of the parish. The tea room and restaurant occupy the building today.

The Route

Leave the war memorial and Market Square and walk over the cobbled car park into Market Place. At a road junction by the police station continue ahead, passing a road signpost for Sutton Cheney. Along this part of the road are some wonderful cottages which date back to the 18th century. Ignore a public footpath signpost on the right to come to the first gate along the gated road to Sutton Cheney.

Proceed through the gate, ensuring that you fasten it afterwards as cattle graze by the roadside. Sutton Lane is extremely quiet as very little traffic uses this highway. There is a very wide, grassy verge to walk along with many local people using this road to exercise their dogs. After a quarter of a mile, if you look carefully to your left you should be able to see Hercules Monument in Bosworth Park.

Ignore the public footpath signpost that leads to the Battle of Bosworth Country Park after a further quarter of a mile and continue to enjoy the gated road that snakes its way through some stunning countryside. Pass through the second gate along the road, now heading uphill on Bosworth Road. From the top of this hill there is a

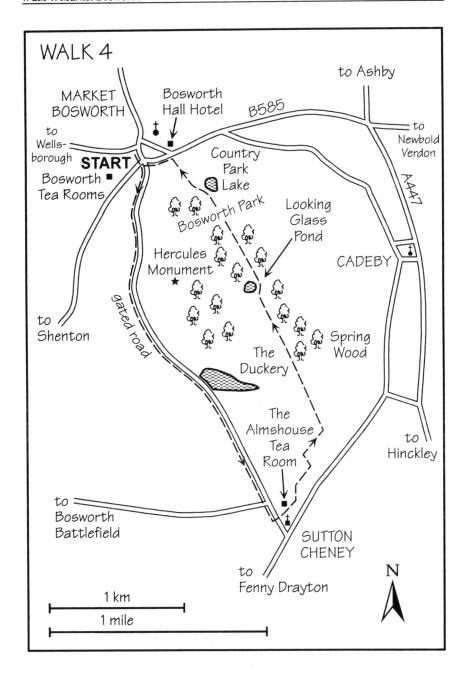

WALK 4

MARKET BOSWORTH

Bosworth Hall Hotel

to Ashby

B585

to Wellsborough

START

Bosworth Tea Rooms

to Newbold Verdon

A447

Country Park Lake

Bosworth Park

Looking Glass Pond

Hercules Monument

CADEBY

to Shenton

gated road

Spring Wood

The Duckery

The Almshouse Tea Room

to Hinckley

to Bosworth Battlefield

SUTTON CHENEY

to Fenny Drayton

N

1 km

1 mile

magical view of Sutton Cheney and its church set in fine, pastoral surroundings.

At the road junction walk ahead towards the village as far as St James's Church. Turn left at a public footpath signpost adjacent to the church and the path leads you to the entrance to The Almshouse. Do call at the tea rooms and drink in the surroundings – it is superb. When thoroughly refreshed, continue along the grassy path to a yellow-topped waymarker post and public footpath signpost.

Cross the field as directed by the signpost to a large hedge gap. Look for a path that crosses the next field – shown by a Leicestershire Round symbol. However, about halfway across, turn left, heading for a yellow-topped waymarker post in the far hedge. Turn right along a wide field perimeter path to arrive at the next waymarker post. Turn left as shown, still following the Leicestershire Round symbol, to cross the next field diagonally. You then reach a junction of footpaths where you need to ignore the path off to the right.

Continue ahead once again on a wide grassy track, walking alongside a hedge. Ahead of you is Spring Wood. When you reach a stream at the Duckery, walk alongside the pretty wood. After 400 metres you come to the beautiful farmhouse at Woodhouse Farm, where a pair of stiles need to be climbed in quick succession. A very pleasant, tree-lined grassy path brings you to the next stile then entry into Bosworth Park.

Go past Looking Glass Pond on the obvious path, perhaps lingering here and there to enjoy the grand views. After a quarter of a mile of superb woodland walking you will encounter a wooden swing gate. Entry through this gate offers you the chance to explore the arboretum. Walk along the resurfaced path, left, following round all too quickly to the lake. After perhaps pausing to feed the ducks with any leftover sandwiches, take the gravelled path away from the arboretum and woodland area through the country park to the road by Bosworth Hall Hotel. Turn left along the park road as far as the road junction, then turn right to return to the car park at The Square and war memorial.

```
Walk 5. Shenton
```

Route: Shenton Hall – Whitemoors Antiques and Crafts Centre – Ashby Canal – Sutton Cheney Wharf – Ambion Wood – Bosworth Battlefield – Shenton Hall.

Start: Shenton Hall, Bosworth Road, Shenton. GR 387004

Distance: 5 miles

Maps: OS Landranger 140 Leicester and Coventry area, OS Pathfinders 893 Tamworth, 914 Nuneaton and 915 Hinckley and Earl Shilton.

Terrain: Flat, open walking across grassy fields. Pleasant towpath by Ashby Canal. Steady climb over Ambion Hill, Bosworth Battlefield.

Public Transport: None

By Car: Shenton may be reached by the A444 or A447 then the B585 to Market Bosworth. The village is clearly signposted along minor roads from the B585.

The Tea Shop

There have been tea rooms at Whitemoors Antiques and Crafts Centre since 1984. Originally Whitemoors Tea Rooms were located in the old farmhouse building with teas being served out of the kitchen window to tables in the courtyard on Sunday afternoons. Today, the proprietress, Joanne Dimblebee, runs a spacious tea room in a converted barn opposite.

After browsing at antiques, refresh yourself in the relaxing ambience of Whitemoors. The menu consists of delicious home-made teas, cakes and savouries. Light lunches are also served daily with special facilities for parties by prior arrangement. On a busy day there is plenty of room to enjoy your 'poison'. The decor is most appealing with beautiful paintings hanging on the walls. The tables are made of antique wood and complement the traditional appeal of the tea rooms.

Opening Hours: 10.30 – 17.00 Monday to Saturday (including bank holidays). 10.00 – 18.00 Sundays. Telephone 01455 212981

Whitemoors Antiques and Crafts Centre

The Whitemoors Antiques and Crafts Centre in the medieval village of Shenton was opened in 1984. The centre is close to the spot where Richard III fell at the Battle of Bosworth. Surrounding the gravelled courtyard is a carefully restored collection of buildings dating back several centuries which originally belonged to Whitemoors Farm. Inside the buildings are various galleries brimming with a selection of fascinating contemporary crafts, antiques, curios, books, objets d'art and the random bric-a-brac of the past two centuries. Static displays include what is probably the Midland's widest collection of beautiful crystal paperweights. Take a stroll through the landscaped gardens, which are maintained by volunteers and where, it is said, on a still day you can still hear the sounds of the battle drifting across the river. Telephone 01455 212250 for further details.

Shenton

A most attractive village close to the Warwickshire border, three miles south-west of Market Bosworth. There are two notable buildings in this private village with a pretty stream flowing through the centre. Shenton Hall was built of brick and dressed with stone in 1629, while the church of St John the Evangelist opposite the hall was built in the late 19th century.

Ashby Canal

The Ashby-de-la-Zouch canal runs from Marston Junction near Bedworth to its current terminus north of Snarestone, passing through attractive countryside. It dates from 1795, and was built originally to transport coal from the mines in North West Leicestershire to many Midlands towns. There are no locks, which is unusual for a canal, as it follows the natural levels of the land. Today, no freight is transported along the waterway but it is very popular with holiday narrow boats and walkers who follow the towpath.

Battle of Bosworth Field and Country Park

On 22nd August 1485, the decisive battle of the Wars of the Roses took place at Bosworth Field between the armies of Richard III and Henry Tudor. This fateful encounter ended with Richard, King of

The Ashby Canal near Sutton Cheney Wharf

England, and last of the Yorkist kings being killed in the battle and Henry, by his triumph, being crowned Henry VII. It brought an end to the feuding of 30 years between the great houses of York and Lancaster. The death of Richard can be seen to mark the end of the Middle Ages as the Tudor era began.

There is a self-guided battle trail of about one and three-quarter miles which takes you around the battlefield, passing the command posts of Richard III and Henry Tudor. The illustrated guide boards placed along the trail give graphic details of each stage of the battle.

In the visitors' centre, opened on 22nd June 1985, in the quincentenary year of the Battle of Bosworth, is an exhibition and film theatre. Here you can walk down a medieval street to discover the sights and sounds of life at that time. The film theatre shows an extract from the famous film of Richard III plus a short, specially commissioned cartoon about the battle. There is also a book and gift shop as well as the Bosworth Buttery Cafeteria, which sells home-made cakes, sandwiches and hot and cold snacks. The country park, which includes the battlefield, is open all year round, while details of the battlefield visitors' centre opening times can be obtained by telephoning 01455 290429.

The Route

From Shenton Hall, walk along Bosworth Road, passing the church, to the road junction by the pretty stream. Turn left along Main Street and head towards Whitemoors for 300 metres to reach Whitemoors Antiques and Crafts Centre. If you fancy an early cup of tea or coffee, why not call at the tea rooms? Continue along the road out of the village, ignoring a double footpath signpost on the right. In a further 200 metres, turn left at a public footpath signpost to join a track.

The track runs alongside a most charming wood then, after passing through a double metal gate, joins a wide field perimeter path. The route is waymarked by special battlefield markers which are used only in the area around Bosworth Field. Climb a double stile then follow a narrow field path across an arable field to the next site. Bear slightly right over the next field and from here you should see the flag flying on the battlefield.

At Apple Orchards Farm pass to the left of the farmhouse, following the waymarker posts and directional arrows. Climb a stile then a two bar fence to walk over a grassy field to reach the Fenny Drayton to Sutton Cheney road. From here there are superb views of the countryside all around, while in the distance is the church spire of Stoke Golding.

Go left along the road for 250 metres to the road junction. Turn right on to Shenton Lane, walking ahead as far as the bridge of the Ashby Canal. On the canal bridge is an Ambion Way footpath signpost and here you need to join the towpath of the canal in the direction of Sutton Wharf. The Ambion Way is a circular walk of eight miles around Hinckley. It follows the Ashby Canal from Hinckley to Sutton Wharf before returning over arable and pasture fields to Richmond Park. There are three separate starting points for this walk.

Pass beneath bridge number 30, where a well-walked towpath follows close to the edge of the canal. Do keep your eyes and ears open as this canal makes a natural habitat for all kinds of birds and small animals. After three-quarters of a mile of pleasant waterside walking you reach a footpath signpost at a junction of paths. Con-

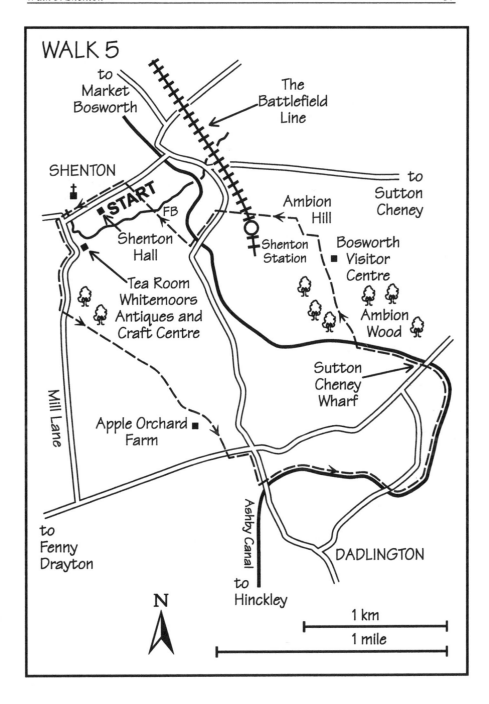

WALK 5

to Market Bosworth

The Battlefield Line

SHENTON

START

FB

Shenton Hall

Tea Room Whitemoors Antiques and Craft Centre

Ambion Hill

Shenton Station

to Sutton Cheney

Bosworth Visitor Centre

Ambion Wood

Mill Lane

Apple Orchard Farm

Sutton Cheney Wharf

to Fenny Drayton

Ashby Canal

to Hinckley

DADLINGTON

N

1 km

1 mile

tinue ahead along the canal, ignoring the Ambion Way and the Leicestershire Round footpath to Hinckley. Go beneath bridge 33, continuing along the towpath, enjoying the open views, until you arrive at Sutton Wharf.

Cross over the road bridge to rejoin the canal on the opposite bank at Sutton Cheney Wharf. If you fancy a trip on the waterbus as far as the Battlefield Bridge and return, why not break your walk and enjoy a scenic ride along the canal? To continue the walk, a swing gate allows you to join a gravelled path that leads you into Ambion Wood in due course. This is a private wood and you are asked to keep to the waymarked path.

At the end of Ambion Wood pass through two gates in fairly quick succession to enter the country park. The visitors' centre can now be visited then you need to join the Battle Trail to Shenton Station and King Richard's Field. A gravelled path takes you uphill on to Ambion Hill. From here there are magnificent views to saviour, especially towards Market Bosworth. Continue over Bosworth Field, where the battle raged in 1485, and along the Battle Trail to reach Shenton Station.

Cross the battlefield railway line with care, then turn left along the road. After crossing the bridge over Ashby Canal, turn right at a public footpath signpost by The Lodge. Walk along a farm track to a stile then continue ahead as directed by the waymarker posts. From here a striking view of Shenton Hall is enjoyed. Cross over the stream where a pretty parkland path brings you to a wooden gate. Turn left along the road back into the village of Shenton and the starting point of the walk at Shenton Hall.

Walk 6. Wistow

Route: Wistow Garden Centre – Newton Harcourt – Grand Union Canal – Kilby – Foston – Arnesby Lodge Farm – Wistow Tea Rooms.

Start: Wistow Garden Centre, Wistow, near Great Glen, Leicester. GR 639958

Distance: 7½ miles

Maps: OS Landranger 140 Leicester and Coventry area and OS Pathfinder 916 Wigston and Kibworth Beauchamp.

Terrain: Mainly flat walking along canal towpath, good footpaths and bridleways. Small amount of road walking.

Public Transport: Regular bus service from Leicester to Kilby and Fleckney, and Fox Cub service to Great Glen via Wistow. Both services operated by Midland Fox.

By Car: Wistow is located seven miles south of Leicester, between the A5199 and the A6, on the road from Kilby to Kibworth. Parking is available at the large car park, Wistow Garden Centre.

The Tea Shop

Wistow Tea Rooms are leased from Wistow Garden Centre and situated adjacent to the car park. The tea rooms have been open since 1977, the same length of time as the garden centre. Over the years the establishment has seen a number of proprietors, with Mrs Denise Dilkes having taken over in 1997. Originally the tea rooms were converted from an old chicken hut belonging to Wistow Farm.

There are 12 tables inside the tea rooms with a further eight tables outside. A full-time, qualified chef is in residence and this allows the menu to have a wide selection of cooked 'goodies' for consumption. Available on certain days are 'chef's special' lunches, while throughout the week lunches and cream teas are always served. Do try the Stilton, Celery and Walnut quiche or the Wistow Cream Tea – both reasonably priced. Speciality teas and wine served by the glass can be enjoyed with your meal. As you would expect, the home-made cakes are baked on the premises, while fresh cream cakes are brought in daily. At weekends the tea rooms are extremely busy so do be prepared for a wait – however, you will not be disappointed with the food or service so the wait will be worthwhile.

Opening Hours: 10.00 – 17.00, seven days a week. Telephone 0116 259 3756

Wistow Garden Centre

The garden centre is part of the Wistow Hall Estate owned by Mr Tim Brooks, Lord Lieutenant of Leicestershire. In 1977, after converting many farm buildings into leasable units, the garden centre was opened. The idea came originally from Mr Brooks selling ice creams on Sundays, then also selling plants from a shooting box on the estate. There is plenty to see to suit all the family, especially Leicestershire's only model village – Wistan Le Dale. Situated within the Georgian walled garden, it is built one-eighteenth of actual size. Each building is individually designed and built in a mid-Victorian setting. A model railway runs around this acclaimed model village. The garden centre is open every day except Tuesdays 10.00 – 17.00, no admission charge. Telephone 0116 259 2009.

Wistow

The old village of Wistow has long since disappeared but Wistow Hall remains. The hall, parish church and garden centre, set in beautiful parkland, make up today's Wistow. The church is dedicated to St Wistan, a royal prince of Mercia, who was probably martyred on the site of the church. Dating back to Norman times, the tower was rebuilt in the 15th century and the church was remodelled in 1746. The ancient church is open weekends Easter to September. Wistow Hall was bought by the Halford family in 1603 and was the family home until 1896. It was here that Sir Richard Halford sheltered Charles I after his defeat at the Battle of Naseby in 1645. The monuments of the Halford family can be found in the parish church in the north chapel.

Kilby

Dating back to medieval times, the village once surrounded the church. St Mary Magdalen Church was built in 1858 on the site of an earlier building. The village today is some distance away from the

Wistow Hall from across the lake

church because, it is thought, of the depopulation of the original medieval village. The Grand Union Canal passes by Kilby, linking Market Harborough and Leicester. This is one reason why Kilby has grown into the bustling, popular village it is today.

Foston

Foston is one of Leicestershire's 'lost villages', with a 10th-century church, house and farm remaining. Earthworks of the medieval village mark the site along Foston Road from the A5199. The site of the village was deserted by the end of the 16th century. St Bartholomew's Church stands by Foston House, and has been added to and altered over the centuries. Spend a little time exploring the churchyard, it is most interesting.

The Route

Walk back to the entrance of Wistow Garden Centre car park then turn right along Wistow Road. Pass Wistow Farm on your way to the church. Do carry on a little further for a superb view of Wistow Hall across the lake.

Back at the church, turn left at a public footpath signpost by the church, following the path ahead to a bridge over the River Sence. Continue ahead over the site of the old village, away from the church, to the next footbridge over a brook. Cross and turn left alongside the brook for a short distance before heading for a grey, metal gate in the far right-hand corner of the field. Climb the stile then make for an obvious gate in the hedge ahead. Upon reaching the road, turn right and follow the road uphill into the village of Newton Harcourt.

Just past the tiny, 13th-century church, cross over the road bridge of the Grand Union Canal. Turn right down a flight of steps that leads to the towpath of the canal. Pass beneath bridge number 80, Newton Bridge, following the pleasant towpath to Newton Top Lock. Pass the picturesque lock keeper's cottage and continue to Spinney Lock. Leave the canal at bridge 81. Return over the canal bridge to a public footpath signpost which is partially hidden in the hedge. A yellow-topped waymarker post and arrow shows the way ahead on to a thin path that runs alongside a wooden fence. The public footpath now runs alongside the canal, but on the opposite side to earlier.

Keep a wooden fence to your right as you pass Top Half-Mile Lock to join a tree-lined path. Keep a sharp eye open here as the countryside is teeming with many different species of birds ranging from goldcrests to herons. In 200 metres the path opens out, and at this point a waymarker post shows the route ahead. Climb a number of stiles in quick succession as you pass through two horse paddock fields by a farmhouse.

A farm track now heads away from the farm with waymarker posts dotted along the way. A short, wide grassy path then brings you to a stile in the hedge. Cross the field on a well-used path, heading for the electricity pylon ahead. Go over a footbridge then continue ahead as indicated by the waymarker arrow to a stile set in a hedge. After crossing a wooden footbridge over the River Sence, make for a stile and public footpath signpost at the top of the hill by the road. Do not emerge out on to the road that leads to Kilby, in-

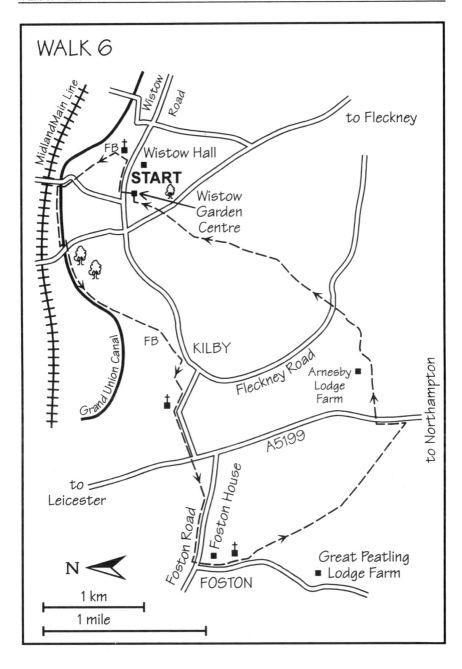

stead, head for a wooden telegraph pole ahead and to the right. Beyond is a stile. After walking across the village park, follow a grassy lane that brings you into the village of Kilby. Turn right along Main Street and walk through the pretty village to come to the A5199 after a quarter of a mile. Cross to the stile opposite, walking over a field path to the next stile. A steady climb brings you to the bridleway and signpost by Foston Road. Turn right along the road. After a quarter of a mile you reach a turn for Foston (gated road).

Pass Foston House then the parish church to find a public bridleway signpost. Turn left on to the track, which is well waymarked, following ahead to reach a bridleway that leads off towards Great Peatling Lodge Farm. Continue on, now walking along a pleasant green track alongside a hedge. At a junction of bridleways, pass through a small, wooden hand gate – now with a hedge on your opposite side. The field path is very well used by local walkers, therefore, it is not difficult to see where the route leads ahead. Pass through an assortment of gates, then just before reaching the A5199 Leicester to Northampton road, look to the right to see the old windmill at Arnesby.

Turn left along the busy A5199 for 250 metres to reach a public bridleway signpost. A farm track leads to Arnesby Lodge Farm, where you need to go to the right through a farm gate by the farm buildings. Immediately past a Dutch barn, turn left over a stile, crossing diagonally over the field to a grey, metal gate. Walk ahead, alongside a hedge, on a grassy track. Bear left on the obvious path to come to a wooden gate. Turn left to a black, metal gate then follow around the field perimeter to reach Fleckney Road.

Cross to the small hand gate opposite to where a public bridleway signpost points the way. Pass through a wooden gate near to Kilby Grange Farm and climb to the brow of the hill over to your right. There is a fine view of the City of Leicester and the hills of Charnwood beyond. Turn left along a wide field path that now stretches out ahead. Go beneath the electricity transmission lines on the very obvious track passing Kilby Lodge.

At the road, turn left and continue for 50 metres, over a cattle grid, to locate a public bridleway signpost. A thin path leads alongside a small wood, and in about 100 metres a side entrance into Wistow Garden Centre will be found. Turn right into the garden centre, the tea rooms and car park are only a short distance away.

Walk 7. Countesthorpe

Route: Glebe Garden Centre – Countesthorpe – Hospital Lane – Blaby – Glen Parva – Grand Union Canal – Countesthorpe – Glebe Garden Centre Tea Room.

Start: Glebe Garden Centre, Foston Road, Countesthorpe. GR 593960

Distance: 6 miles

Maps: OS Landranger 140 Leicester and Coventry area and OS Pathfinder 915 Hinckley and Earl Shilton.

Terrain: Easy walking along clear footpaths and tracks. Towpath by Grand Union Canal very picturesque. No steep climbs.

Public Transport: A very frequent Leicester – Countesthorpe – South Wigston service runs Monday to Saturday, operated by Midland Fox. There is a more limited Sunday service.

By Car: Use A5199 Leicester to Northampton road or A426 Leicester to Lutterworth road from Leicester city centre. Follow signs for Countesthorpe from either of these roads once through Wigston and Blaby respectively. Parking is available at the garden centre car park.

The Tea Shop

Tucked away at the rear of Glebe Garden Centre is Mr Beanbags coffee shop. What a great name! Mr Carl Durham owns this café, and also a Mr Beanbags shop in Oadby. Jenny Gorman manages this pleasant little establishment, which has been in existence only since 1995. Prior to being a coffee shop it was just a storeroom for the garden centre. The coffee shop is a separate entity to the garden centre.

There is room for 40 to enjoy Jenny's delicious menu, including a wide range of sandwiches, soups, snacks, savouries and beverages. All cakes are home-made but do try Mr Beanbags' special: a toasted tea cake and a cup of ground coffee or a pot of royalty tea. The tea room's reputation for its tea cakes is well-deserved. If peckish, bite into a hub cap bap with a filling chosen from ham, beef, cheddar or prawns. The cream tea is good value consisting of a fruit scone, butter, jam, cream and a pot of tea. The coffee shop is tastefully decorated with blue chairs complimenting the pine tables, and the aroma of fresh coffee filling the air.

Opening Hours: 10.45 – 16.30 Monday to Saturday, 10.30 – 16.30 on Sundays. Telephone 0116 277 9465

Glebe Garden Centre

Opened in 1974, the garden centre caters for all types of gardeners. It is owned by Bernard Hanraads and Mary Knifton who really make you feel at home when pottering about in their garden. The garden centre is on one level and welcomes wheelchairs. From October to December there is a really good Christmas display with 12 Christmas trees decorated in different styles – well worth seeing.

Countesthorpe

Countesthorpe is situated six miles south of Leicester with a population of 6700. The village name is derived from the 11th century, when the area formed part of the marriage dowry of Countess Judith, niece of William the Conqueror – 'thorpe' meaning 'land'. The parish church of St Andrew dates to 1220, and was restored in 1840 and 1907. The tower, which is 14th century, still remains. The village

Which way to go? Look out for this footbridge near Countesthorpe!

has many fine half-timbered houses, with one dating back to the 15th century. In Peatling Road there is an example of a Leicestershire mud house. As well as being a commuter village for Leicester, Countesthorpe has a number of small knitwear factories employing local people.

Blaby

The village of Blaby has a thriving shopping centre which serves the district. Over the last 25 years, Blaby has expanded in size considerably, bringing its population to 6500. Much of the older part of the village has been designated as a conservation area. It includes the 12th-century parish church of All Saints, a timbered inn built about 1485 and the village green nearby.

The Route

Leave the car park of the garden centre and turn right on to Foston Road, walking into Countesthorpe village. Cross Leicester Road to Buckingham Road then turn right immediately into Judith Drive. At the end of the short road follow round to the right into Edgeley Road then around to the left to reach a turning for The Elms. At the end of the road is a public footpath signpost and a wooden stile which needs to be climbed.

An obvious path takes you over a grassy field to a bridge over the old railway line. Cross, then pass through a metal farm gate at the end of a track. The well-used track runs parallel to a hedge, with the village of Blaby seen ahead. A wooden swing gate allows you to tread a grassy path that cuts through an arable field to the next wooden gate. The walk along the path still continues ahead as before to bring you to Hospital Lane.

Walk along the road for 400 metres to the entrance signpost to Blaby village. Turn right along a grassy track, ignoring the permissive path after 200 metres. The track switches to the opposite side of the hedge and there is a pleasant view of Long Walk Wood. Upon reaching a small, wooden swing gate, do not go through, but turn left along the track towards the wood. Pass through the right-hand swing gate at the entrance to the wood to join a field path. Walk adjacent to a wooden fence, then head to the right of Blaby church to reach the road at Hall Farm.

Turn right and walk along Church Street for 20 metres before going left on to Wigston Road. After 25 metres, go along an alleyway by a public footpath signpost. The 'all weather' path wends and winds its way to a large, iron bridge that spans the River Sence. Cross and remain on the resurfaced path that veers off to the right, ignoring all other local paths. Turn left through a black, iron kissing gate, continuing ahead to the next kissing gate, then the B582.

This road is busy and you must take care as you walk to the right towards South Wigston through Glen Parva. A wonderful sight awaits of Glen Parva Manor (built about 1452), where it is thought that King Charles I stayed after the Battle of Naseby. The manor house today is a public house and restaurant but retains much of its previous look. Continue along Little Glen Road to reach a public footpath signpost just before the canal bridge.

A short path leads to the canal towpath by bridge number 94, Little Glen Bridge. Turn right along the towpath of the Grand Union Canal. There are majestic views of the rural surroundings to enjoy. After three-quarters of a mile you may fancy a break at Crow Mill Picnic Site where the Crow Mill Way can be explored. Opened in 1991 by Blaby District Council, this area is developing into an interesting nature reserve on the site of the disused railway line.

Continue along the towpath, passing beneath Crow Mill's Bridge (number 62), then go by Ervin's Lock and leave South Wigston behind. After passing beneath Pochin's Bridge and Knight's Bridge in quick succession, leave the canal at Double Rail Lock. Climb the stile by the yellow-topped waymarker post to join a well-used field path that leads ahead to a footbridge over a stream. Cross the next field, as before, to reach a second footbridge. Once over, follow a path that runs alongside the stream to a third footbridge and a junction of paths. On the footbridge is a myriad of arrows to confuse the situation. Do not cross the bridge but continue on, along a path which is probably overgrown in summer.

Walk alongside the sewage works then turn right as shown by a yellow-topped waymarker post. Upon encountering the access track into the works, turn left. At the entrance to the sewage works, turn right, and continue along a field perimeter path next to a hedge. Turn left over a stile in a fence then turn right, still following the field perimeter path to the top of the field by Leicester Road. Follow the field around to the left and past the rugby club to return to Countesthorpe. At Foston Road turn left, retracing your footsteps to the garden centre and well-earned refreshments at Mr Beanbags.

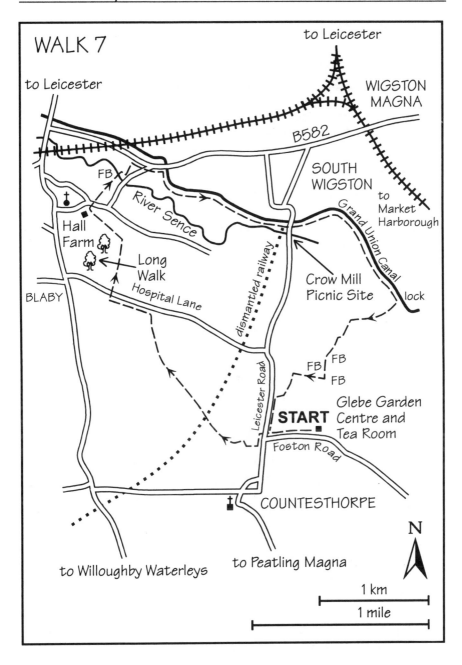

WALK 7

to Leicester

to Leicester

WIGSTON MAGNA

B582

FB

SOUTH WIGSTON

to Market Harborough

River Sence

Hall Farm

Long Walk

Hospital Lane

BLABY

Crow Mill Picnic Site

Grand Union Canal

lock

dismantled railway

Leicester Road

FB | FB
FB

START

Glebe Garden Centre and Tea Room

Foston Road

COUNTESTHORPE

to Willoughby Waterleys

to Peatling Magna

N

1 km

1 mile

```
┌─────────────────────────────────────────────────────────────┐
│                                                               │
│                  Walk 8. Ullesthorpe                          │
│                                                               │
└─────────────────────────────────────────────────────────────┘
```

Route: Ullesthorpe – Claybrooke Parva – Claybrooke Mill – Lodge Farm – Leire – Jubilee Walk – Ullesthorpe Golf Course – Ullesthorpe.

Start: The Swan Inn, Main Street, Ullesthorpe. GR 505877

Distance: 5½ miles

Maps: OS Landranger 140 Leicester and Coventry area and OS Pathfinder 936 Lutterworth.

Terrain: Good walking along well-defined field footpaths and tracks. Dismantled railway line at Leire is now a nature trail, no steep climbs to trouble you.

Public Transport: A fairly regular bus service between Leicester and Rugby, operated by Pam's Coaches, calls at Ullesthorpe. No Sunday service.

By Car: Ullesthorpe can be reached by using the A5 from Hinckley to High Cross then the B577. Alternatively, the M1 to Lutterworth and, following signs for Bitteswell, approach Ullesthorpe on the B577 from the opposite direction. Parking may be available at The Swan Inn, please ask first. Otherwise, park where you can in the village.

The Tea Shop

It was in 1992 that Ian and Ruth Tallis took charge of Ullesthorpe Garden and Aquatic Centre, opening the Conservatory Tea Room soon after. James Bailey runs the tea room, which is situated to the rear of the garden centre in a light and spacious conservatory. Inside are 10 tables which can seat up to 40 people, while outside are a further nine tables that can seat an additional 36 to 40 diners. Whilst enjoying a cream tea there is a beautiful landscaped garden to admire, and in the summer the conservatory is a sun trap – as is the outside patio.

All cakes are home-made with some pastries being supplied by a local bakery. If you have an appetite after the walk, try the Gardener's Lunch. Choose from ham, turkey or corned beef, served with a generous salad, also including egg, cheese, home-made coleslaw and a roll and butter – a veritable feast! The tea room welcomes walkers calling in for morning coffee or tea and cakes. If you are short of time, ring your order ahead and they will prepare it for when you arrive. The tea room also offers a take-away service.

Note: This tea room is not on the walk. It is three-quarters of a mile from the centre of Ullesthorpe village, in the direction of Lutterworth.

Opening Hours: Monday to Saturday 9.00 – 17.00 (16.00 in the winter). Sunday 10.30 – 16.00.

Ullesthorpe Garden and Aquatic Centre

Nestling in the picturesque South Leicestershire countryside, local people with long memories will recall that this garden centre was previously named The Oasis. The present owners renamed and revamped the site! There is something of interest for everyone: admiring the wide range of fish in the Aquatic Centre, perusing the gardening books on display, lingering in Pets' Corner with the children or wandering through the delightful landscaped grounds. The garden centre is unrivalled in its selection of indoor and outdoor plants, all attractively displayed. A special feature is the shrub garden, which is laid out in ornamental style with a fish pond complete with waterfall and bridge.

Ullesthorpe

A large village within the parish of Claybrooke Parva, Ullesthorpe is unusual in having no Anglican church of its own. Ullesthorpe dates back to the Domesday Book, which records that a mill existed here in 1086. The shell of the Tower Windmill remains owned privately. In 1890 the windmill was struck by lightning and its sails were set alight. In the Second World War, it was further damaged by a bomb which exploded close by. The 17th-century Ullesthorpe Court Manor House has been converted into a hotel and golf complex with extensive conference facilities.

Claybrooke Parva

Claybrooke Parva is the smaller of the two villages that make up the district of Claybrooke. Curiously, the large village of Claybrooke Magna has no church. Instead, a fine 14th-century building, con-

Ullesthorpe village is full of beautiful old buildings

structed of pink sandstone, stands in stately isolation in Claybrooke Parva. Of special note is the decorated tracery of the windows.

About half a mile to the east of the village is Claybrooke Mill, which is passed on the walk. This mill is the only working watermill in Leicestershire and retains much of the original milling machinery. Stoneground flour is still made here, but the mill is private and walkers must keep to the recognised path through the mill buildings.

The Route

The Swan Inn car park is situated at the rear of the pub, off Main Street. Commence the walk by turning right on to Main Street and follow the road round a double bend, heading for Claybrooke Parva. Go downhill out of Ullesthorpe village, making for the unusual-shaped church in Claybrooke Parva ahead. Cross the road bridge that straddles the brook then pass the riding stables as you enter the village. Just before a bend in the road turn right at a Leicestershire Round signpost to Claybrooke Magna Mill.

A narrow path by a wire fence stretches ahead and brings you to a group of farm buildings. Join a farm track, marked appropriately by a yellow-topped waymarker post and blue arrow, and follow to reach a large pair of grey, metal gates. Go through the left-hand gate and on to a small, wooden gate in front of you. Cross the next field, as directed by the waymarker arrow, to a large hedge gap. Continue along the field perimeter path to a wooden swing gate then move over to join an obvious track. Cross the next field diagonally to a sturdy wooden footbridge at Claybrooke Mill.

The route through the mill yard is well marked. You need to make for a large bridge to the rear of the outbuildings. Cross the mill race, turn right, and pass through a wooden gate to rejoin the Leicestershire Round footpath ahead. At first follow alongside a hedge then where the hedge turns right at an angle, cross the field in the direction of the line of wooden telegraph posts. Turn right through a hedge gap then walk along the enclosed path towards the left. In summer this path may well be overgrown, but it is quite passable. A wooden swing gate allows you to enter a beautiful wood, which is home to the local scouting group, where a wide woodland path brings you to a road.

Turn left along the road and proceed for 200 metres to a T-junction at the brow of the hill. Opposite is a public footpath signpost where a stile ensures that you can join an obvious field footpath ahead. Head for the corner of the field and a yellow-topped waymarker post. Continue over the next field in the same manner, now making for the white-fronted building at Lodge Farm. Upon reaching the farm gate, turn left and go along the road for 50 metres to locate a public footpath signpost.

Climb an awkward, small fence to join a field perimeter path that is adjacent to a very tall hedge. Where the boundary hedge turns left, climb a well-hidden stile and cross the next field diagonally to a small fence set in a hedge. Go over the next field to a gap in the hedge opposite and join a field perimeter path that follows alongside a hedge. Leave the hedge when it turns to the left and continue slightly diagonally across the field to a wooden post and yellow waymarker arrow. Turn left on to the well-trodden path which runs along the embankment of the dismantled railway trackbed. You soon emerge on Leire playing fields, which you cross, passing the children's play area.

A path goes down to the old railway trackbed, which at Leire has been converted into a nature trail called the Jubilee Walk, opened in May 1986. Turn right along the thin path that weaves along the flat trackbed – either side of the path the embankment has returned to its natural environment with many species of wild flowers and plants gracing the slopes. It is amazing how nature can return so soon after the railway line closed. The Jubilee Walk unfortunately concludes at the Frolesworth road bridge. There are many notices attached to the bridge advising users that the next part of the old railway line is private and a steep path leads you up the side of the embankment and out on to the road.

Turn right on the road bridge and walk ahead for 100 metres to find a public footpath signpost in the hedge. Cross the field to the opposite corner as shown by the waymarker arrow on the yellow-topped waymarker post. Pass through a hedge gap then in 20 metres turn right, climbing the embankment by turning right at a yellow-topped waymarker post. Go down the embankment to a stile. A grassy path alongside the old railway line leads ahead to Ullesthorpe and is surrounded by attractive gardens and golf fairways.

Climb an iron ladder stile adjacent to a dog paddle. Join the path that hugs close to the old railway embankment and crosses the golf course. The route is marked by yellow-topped waymarker posts, but you are always in danger from golf balls so do listen out for a call of 'four'. At the end of the golf course climb a stile then follow an enclosed alleyway to Mill Road, Ullesthorpe. Pass the remains of Tower Windmill to reach the road junction. Turn right on to Main Street, passing by the post office to complete the walk at the Swan Inn.

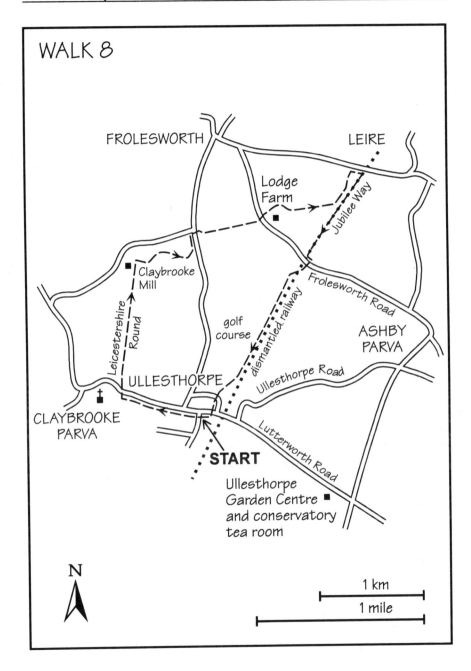

WALK 8

FROLESWORTH

LEIRE

Lodge Farm

Jubilee Way

Claybrooke Mill

Leicestershire Round

golf course

Frolesworth Road

dismantled railway

ASHBY PARVA

ULLESTHORPE

Ullesthorpe Road

CLAYBROOKE PARVA

Lutterworth Road

START

Ullesthorpe Garden Centre and conservatory tea room

N

1 km

1 mile

Walk 9. Kibworth Beauchamp

Route: Beauchamps – Debdale Grange – Smeeton Hill – Saddington – Fleckney – Kibworth Beauchamp – Beauchamps.

Start: Beauchamps, High Street, Kibworth Beauchamp. GR 681936

Distance: 8 miles

Maps: OS Landranger 141 Kettering, Corby and surrounding area, OS Pathfinder 916 Wigston and Kibworth Beauchamp.

Terrain: Excellent paths and tracks over undulating countryside. Steady climb up Smeeton Hill, where there are panoramic views.

Public Transport: A frequent Leicester to Market Harborough service calls at Kibworth Beauchamp (operated by Midland Fox).

By Car: The village of Kibworth Beauchamp is approached by the A6 from either Leicester of Market Harborough. There is a small, free car park in the village. If full, park where you can in the side roads or on High Street.

The Tea Shop

Beauchamps is a tea room with a difference. Walking into the shop you are greeted with a delicatessen which has a fine choice of home-made preserves and savouries. Do try the Victoria sandwich cake – it is scrumptious. At the rear of the shop is the tea room, tastefully decorated with many framed prints on the walls. There is also a violin and an old tennis racquet exhibited. Tall plants in the tea room combine to help create an ambience that is unrivalled for miles around.

The proprietor, Mr T Alan Palmer, ensures that the tea room has a wide range of snacks and sandwiches each day, coupled with a good choice of coffees. Everything is reasonably priced and at lunch time hot food is available and suitable for all. Beauchamps is the complete caterers. They will arrange the food for weddings, anniversaries, christenings, dinner parties, barbecues and even corporate entertainment for 5000 people at a weekend event.

Opening Hours: Monday to Friday 08.30 – 17.30, Saturdays 08.30 – 17.00. Closed all day Sunday. Telephone 0116 279 3208

Beauchamps tea shop is found at the rear of the delicatessan

Kibworth

Situated eight miles south-east of Leicester, Kibworth consists of two villages and not one as the eye first appears to see. Kibworth Harcourt lies to the east of the A6 while Kibworth Beauchamp is found to the west. Both villages share one church, the parish church of St Wilfred.

Kibworth Beauchamp, a most attractive village, is the larger of the two. The church dates from the second half of the 14th century with the tower having been rebuilt between 1832 and 1836 after the collapse of the spire. At that time a clock was also added to the church, being incorporated into the tower. It is signed by John Harbury of West Haddon and dated 1834.

The streets of Kibworth Beauchamp contain a wealth of interesting buildings. The oldest house is the Manor House on High Street, which was built in the 16th century. It is an H-shaped Tudor house, designed as a compliment to King Henry. In 1913 the stables were added and a decorative clock turret was built. This can be seen at the start of the walk.

Fleckney

A fast-growing village, Fleckney still manages to retain its own distinct charm and character. An industrial village, it has had a long association with the Leicestershire knitting industry – the well-known hosiery firm of Wolsey Ltd of Leicester was founded here in 1860. Today, knitwear has been joined by other light industries including plastics and footwear.

Fleckney has many footpaths and bridleways radiating from the centre of the village. The Grand Union Canal flows to the north-east and there are pleasant walks that take you to this popular waterway.

The Route

Start at Beauchamps on High Street and with the tea shop on your right walk along this road to the roundabout. Continue ahead, still on High Street, as far as Weir Street. Turn right, then where the road bends to the left, turn right on to a tarmac standing. Here a public footpath signpost will be found near a white gate. Follow a thin path that skirts around the school playing fields to reach a wooden stile.

A field path now leads ahead towards a farm. The route is extremely well waymarked. After crossing a farm road, a junction of footpaths will be encountered. The village of Smeeton Westerby will be noted and you now need to bear slightly left over the next field to a double gate that allows you to cross a wide stream. Bear right towards a tree. After crossing the next field, a bridge over a steam is reached. Follow the obvious field path as far as the bridge across the Grand Union Canal.

Cross and climb a stile to join a field perimeter path that leads uphill to Debdale Grange. Another stile gives access to a grassy field path that brings you to the road. Turn right to walk along the quiet minor road for a quarter of a mile to a public footpath signpost and stile. Turn right over the stile, crossing the short field to another minor road. Opposite is a track which is now followed to its end.

Turn right over the stile, following alongside a hedge below Smeeton Hill. Continue alongside the hedge then descend and climb a hill to the next stile. The path goes around to the left of the field, and you should follow the yellow-topped waymarker posts in this direction. At a junction of footpaths, bear right uphill, now following the Leicestershire Round waymarker discs. At the top of the hill, pause and enjoy the extensive views of the delightful country-

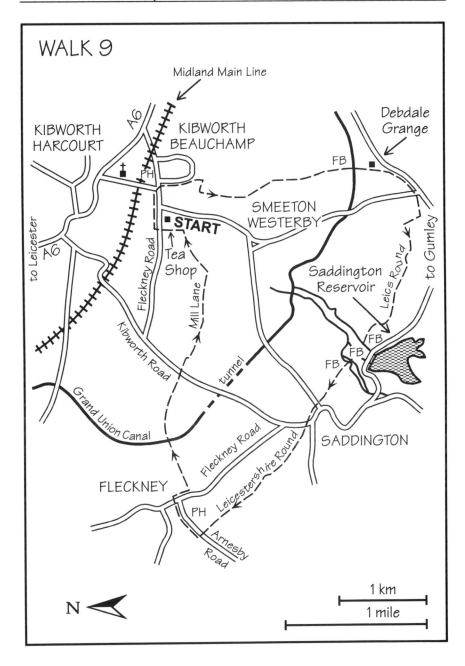

side. Continue ahead with a hedge on your right hand side, now glimpsing for the first time Saddington Reservoir below. The obvious path trundles ahead, with the yellow-topped waymarker posts showing the way. The village of Saddington is seen in the distance perched high on a hill. Go downhill to three bridges in quick succession that allow you to cross three streams. Climb two stiles, then cross two more streams before a steep hill path brings you to Saddington village.

Do not turn left into the village centre but continue ahead, passing Home Farmhouse to reach a footpath at the end of the road. This is still the Leicestershire Round. At a wooden swing gate, bear left over a short field to the road. Cross to the Leicestershire Round footpath signpost opposite that points to Shearsby. After climbing a trio of stiles, bear to the left as shown to pass by a pond. At a farm gate the Leicestershire Round footpath goes off to the left, you make for a new housing estate seen ahead. Turn left on to a farm track to an old building in need of repair. Pass by the entrance into the new housing development, which is part of Fleckney village, and continue ahead on the thin path that now runs alongside the back gardens of many houses. Climb a number of stiles on this well-used path before crossing a stream to reach Arnesby Road, Fleckney.

Turn right into the village, passing the Golden Shield public house then St Nicholas's Church. At the road junction turn right along Fleckney Road then first left into Kibworth Road. Take the next left turn along a short road to a gate. Here join a wide, grassy bridleway that leads to a bridge over the Grand Union Canal. Cross and rejoin the field bridleway that now goes uphill to a gate. Continue ahead to come to Kibworth Road after about 300 metres.

Cross to Mill Lane opposite – a gravelled track. As you walk along the track it becomes rutted, and after heavy rain is liable to be muddy. After three quarters of a mile, a public footpath signpost will be located on the left. Climb the stile then cross the field as indicated by the waymarker posts, heading for the village of Kibworth Beauchamp ahead. At a junction of footpaths, turn left, cross a small bridge and two stiles in quick succession to a swing gate. A short path now brings you to Fleckney Road in Kibworth Beauchamp village.

Turn right along this road, continuing into High Street where Beauchamps will be found in a further 150 metres – a delightful conclusion to a most satisfying walk.

```
┌─────────────────────────────────────────────────────────┐
│                                                           │
│              Walk 10. Saddington                          │
│                                                           │
└─────────────────────────────────────────────────────────┘
```

Route: Saddington – Saddington Lodge Farm – Peashill Farm – Mowsley – Saddington Road – Mowsley Brook – Jacqui's Tea Room – Saddington.

Start: St Helen's Church, Mowsley Road, Saddington. GR 658918

Distance: 5 miles

Maps: OS Landrangers 141 Kettering, Corby and surrounding area and 140 Leicester and Coventry. OS Pathfinders 916 Wigston and Kibworth Beauchamp and 937 Market Harborough.

Terrain: Easy walking across grassy fields on clear footpaths, well-signposted throughout. Quiet section of road walking from Mowsley.

Public Transport: An adequate service between Leicester and Market Harborough calls at Saddington (operated by Woods of Leicester).

By Car: Saddington can either be reached from the A6 Leicester to Market Harborough or A5199 Leicester to Northampton roads. Follow signposts from these roads for the village. Parking is in short supply around the church or in the village.

The Tea Shop

Jacqui's Tea Room at Barford House Farm is situated on Mowsley Road, about a mile from the centre of Saddington village. The tea room is very unusual. It is a purpose-built, wooden chalet (Swiss-style) used solely for weekend teas. Jacqui Skinner has been serving teas here since August 1990, in the beautiful surroundings of an old orchard. The tea room seats 30 inside but hundreds outside on the lawns, and in the restored orchard.

As you would expect, everything is home-made except for the bread, and there is a wonderful selection of cakes and meringues, gateaux, cheese cakes, ice cream sundaes and specials from the board to choose from. Morning coffee, light lunches and afternoon tea including a superb cream tea are also sold. Next to the tea room is a little shop which sells interesting gifts and antiques that is well worth a poke around. Back inside the tastefully decorated tea room, second-hand books are for sale, along with a few guides. Mention

The entrance to Jacqui's tea room near Saddington

must be made of the excellent beverages on offer. Sparkling elder-flower or ginger ale toddy must be tried before leaving. Do allow plenty of time for this visit – you must never rush one of Jacqui's teas, they are too good to hurry.

Opening Hours: 11.00 – 18.00 on Saturdays, Sundays and bank holidays. (Closed Leicester July Fortnight and from Christmas to the first Friday in February.) Telephone 01162 402276

Saddington

Standing on top of a hill, Saddington overlooks some of the finest countryside in the south-west of Leicestershire. Down below in the valley lies Saddington Reservoir, while to the east flows the Grand Union Canal. Here the canal passes through Saddington Tunnel, built in 1797 and half a mile long.

The village has many interesting houses dating to the early 1800s. St Helen's Church was rebuilt in 1872 except for the tower and nave arcades. The oldest part of the church is the south arcade which is 13th century. Probably the best view of the beautiful area is from the car park of the 19th-century Queen's Head public house, where stronger refreshments are available if required.

Mowsley

Mowsley is a small village on the summit of a hill of the same name. It is a pleasant village which is well worth exploring and has a number of buildings dating back to the 18th century. St Nicholas's Church was built around 1300 and restored in 1882 by J L Pearson. As you approach the village on the walk, do look out for the remains of the medieval fishponds about halfway uphill. (See the route for further details.)

The Route

After a visit to St Helen's Church and an exploration of the church-yard, leave the village centre by walking along Mowsley Road as far as a sharp turn to the left. Here a public footpath signpost will be located and a stile. Walk ahead for 20 metres to the next stile and yellow waymarker post.

Climb the stile then turn left and follow alongside a hedge over a

grassy field. Pass two yellow-topped waymarker posts in quick succession in the hedge, walking along an obvious path that crosses
many short fields – all marked by wooden stiles. There are many
lovely views to enjoy of lush, green countryside broken up by woods
and boundary hedges.

At a junction of footpaths, climb two stiles close together then
walk over the field diagonally, aiming for a line of six trees. Pass
through the metal farm gate then continue ahead in the same direction to a yellow-topped waymarker post in the right-hand corner of
the field. Climb the stile then bear right as shown to a double stile,
continuing ahead and passing to the rear of Saddington Lodge Farm.
At the farm track turn left, cross the cattle grid, and pass through the
farmyard to a wide, wooden gate just past the farmhouse.

A grassy track leads to a farm gate then you need to head slightly
right over the field to another gate. Now make for a track ahead. 50
metres along the track, turn left over two field-corner stiles. Climb
uphill as shown by the waymarker, heading for a stile and a yellow-
topped waymarker post to the left of a large oak.

Climb the stile then continue alongside a hedge, passing to the
left of the buildings at Peashill Farm. A stile is hidden in the corner
of the field then you need to go downhill, following a tall hedge to a
farm gate and an adjacent stile. In 150 metres turn right and cross a
stile either side of a ditch. Go over a farm track then continue ahead
by a row of trees and bushes to the next waymarker post.

From this point the village of Mowsley will be seen ahead
perched on top of a tall hill. Climb two stiles at the far end of the field
then make for a farm track that goes downhill then uphill. A short
distance uphill, leave the track and climb a stile. Continue diagonally uphill, noting the fish ponds below. At a junction of footpaths,
climb the stile and an enclosed path leads ahead for 200 metres to
emerge on the road at Mowsley village.

Turn left on to Saddington Road and follow the road through the
pretty village, ensuring that you turn left at a road signpost for Saddington. Pass Mowsley Grange at the end of the village and from
here you will need to tread along the road, which is quiet, for a further half mile before reaching a public footpath signpost where the
road bends slightly to the right.

Pass through the gates to join a pleasant, grassy track that goes off
at an angle to the road, to a stile by a gate. From here there is a mag-

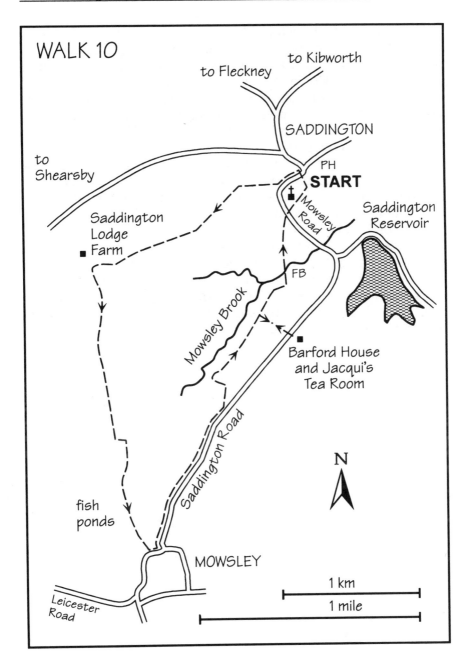

WALK 10

to Fleckney

to Kibworth

SADDINGTON

to Shearsby

PH

START

Mowsley Road

Saddington Lodge Farm

Saddington Reservoir

FB

Mowsley Brook

Barford House and Jacqui's Tea Room

Saddington Road

N

fish ponds

MOWSLEY

1 km

1 mile

Leicester Road

nificent view of Saddington village far in the distance. Turn left along the field perimeter to a stream, then turn right at a yellow-topped waymarker post. Walk along by Mowsley Brook, climbing stiles which are easily found along the path.

At an obvious junction of footpaths denoted by waymarker arrows on a post, turn right uphill, climbing two stiles to reach the car park for the tea rooms. Turn left along Mowsley Road to the entrance to Jacqui's Tea Room at Barford House in 50 metres. After a delightful stop, to continue with the walk it is a simple case of retracing your footsteps along the path going downhill to the stream. Turn right then continue as before, with the walk still following alongside the steam to reach the wooden footbridge that allows you to cross Saddington Brook.

Follow either of the paths that lead away through a small wood and out into a field. A steady climb by a tall hedge brings you to a stile. Cross the next field to Mowsley Road then cross to a track opposite for Manor Farm Riding School and Livery Stables. Follow the track through the stable yard and out on to Mowsley Road by the church to conclude the walk.

Walk 11. Market Harborough

Route: Aldwinckles – Six Packs Inn – Grand Union Canal Arm – Great Bowden Hall – Market Harborough – Aldwinckles.

Start: Aldwinckles Coffee Shop, Aldwinckles Yard off Church Street, Market Harborough. GR 733874

Distance: 5½ miles

Maps: OS Landranger 141 Kettering, Corby and surrounding area, OS Pathfinder 937 Market Harborough.

Terrain: Good, clear footpaths and tracks. Wide towpath by canal. One fairly steep climb at Great Bowden.

Public Transport: Market Harborough Station is served by frequent trains from Nottingham, Derby, Leicester and London St Pancras. There is a good bus service between Northampton and Leicester, including Sundays, that calls at Market Harborough. It is operated by Midland Fox or Stagecoach (United Counties).

By Car: The town is well connected to the national road and motorway networks. The M1 passes to the west with the A427 linking Market Harborough to the motorway. From Leicester use the A6 then B6047 to the town centre. The A14 has improved east-west communications by linking the M1/M6, junction 19 at Catthorpe, to the A1. There is parking at The Commons long-stay car park (free) in the town centre.

The Tea Shop

In May 1987, John Chesterfield opened Aldwinckles Coffee Shop in Aldwinckles Yard. Since that date the tea shop has gone from strength to strength, due, no doubt, to the excellent cuisine that it offers. The courtyard was originally a group of cottages that were converted into flats and offices, apart from this building which was purchased by the proprietor and changed into a coffee shop to his specification. A brick in the wall has the year 1796 inscribed and the original beams and floor are retained. Although the coffee shop is quite small, there are plenty of tables available on two levels and in summer tables are put out in the courtyard.

The food is of the highest standard, ranging from toasties and snacks to more substantial meals such as cottage pie. Scones are home-made with lashings of jam and cream. A selection of teas and coffees are available, all reasonably priced. Aldwinckles is licensed should you require an alcoholic beverage. The complete menu is available all day so why not be daring and indulge those taste buds! The Coffee Shop gets extremely busy in summer so be prepared to wait a short time for a table. However, the wait is worthwhile.

Opening Hours: 09.00 – 17.00, all year round. Not open on Sundays. Telephone 01858 431682.

Market Harborough

As the name implies, Market Harborough has long been a market town. In fact, a market is held three days a week – Tuesday, Friday and Saturday. The town is a medieval settlement – its name being a corruption of Haver Burgh (oat hill). Dating back to the 12th century, it was created as a purpose-built town to attract trade. An interesting way to describe Harborough could be as a medieval 'new town'.

The town has historic links with transport. With the advent of turnpiking, Market Harborough became an important staging post for horse-drawn traffic, borne out by the number of coaching inns that still line the wide High Street. In 1809 the town was linked to the canal network with the Market Harborough arm of the Leicester Line of the Grand Union Canal opening. However, the prosperity of the canal was short-lived for by 1850 the railway had arrived. Transport patterns changed as Market Harborough became the hub of six railway lines linking all the major towns of the East Midlands. Today only one line exists, which is served by Midland Mainline trains between London and Nottingham, Derby and Sheffield via Leicester.

Market Harborough is dominated by the 13th-century parish church of St Dionysius. Its superb spire extends 161 feet (49m) above High Street. The spire is one of the finest in England and is built of smooth, grey limestone. Alongside the church is one of Leicestershire's most unusual buildings. The timber-framed Old Grammar School, with an open ground floor, was built in 1614 to serve as a market place for the weekly butter market. The school above was founded by Robert Smyth and was used until 1892. To-

The 17th century timber-framed grammar school, Market Harborough

day the upstairs building is in continuous use for meetings and exhibitions.

If you have a passion for antiques then you will love Market Harborough. The town has a wide range of antique shops, galleries and old book shops. For details of where to find these shops in the area, please contact the Tourist Information Centre at Pen Lloyds Library for an interesting directory leaflet.

Great Bowden

This is the original settlement associated with Market Harborough. In the late 12th century the daughter settlement of Market Harborough developed within its parish. Great Bowden retains its own identity, although contiguous with Market Harborough. The village is noted for its series of greens around which rows of houses and cottages stand. One green still retains the 19th-century, granite horse trough, erected by the Metropolitan Drinking Fountain and Cattle Trough Association for the welfare of horses.

The Route

From the entrance to Aldwinckles Yard on Church Street, keep the church behind you and walk ahead into High Street then Leicester Road, as far as the former Six Packs Inn, now bricked up. Turn left along the driveway that leads to the canal basin at Market Harborough. It was at the basin in 1950 that the town hosted the first ever British Canal Rally.

The path goes around to the left of the workshops that belong to Harborough Boats to gain access to the canal towpath. On the opposite bank of the canal, beautiful, lawned gardens sweep down to the water's edge. This section of the canal is very popular with swans, moorhens, mallards and coots as well as anglers, with their long carbon fishing rods that straddle the towpath. You may even be lucky to see a kingfisher gliding just above the water.

Ignore the footpath that leads off left by the concrete footbridge. Continue along the towpath as before to reach a farm access road bridge. Cross to the opposite bank then pass beneath Uncle Tom's Bridge, which takes the A6047 over the canal. At this point the canal and towpath widen and it really is a pleasant walk along the tree-lined path. Go beneath Saunt's Bridge (11), and in a further 400 me-

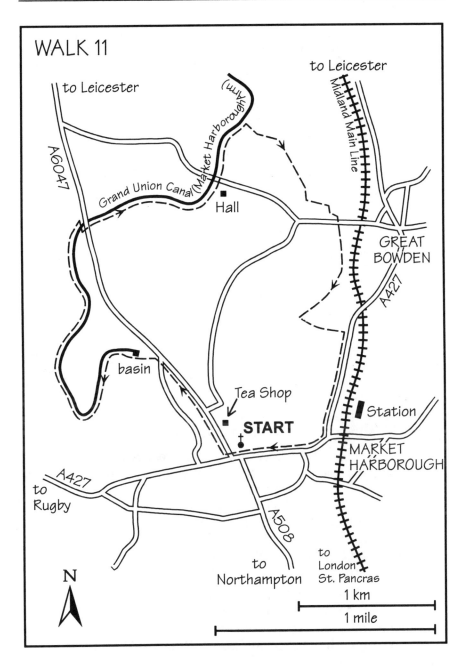

tres Great Bowden Hall will be passed. The hall has now been converted into a new development of luxury mews, houses and apartments, giving owners the opportunity to live in a beautiful setting with established and maintained grounds.

Pass below Bowden Hall Bridge, number 10, continuing ahead on the towpath for a further 200 metres to reach Sedgeley's Bridge (9), where you leave the canal towpath. Turn right over the wooden stile to join a field path, walking ahead in the direction of the yellow waymarker arrow. Pass through a metal gate on to a track. At a junction of footpaths, bear slightly right across a field, heading for a red, metal gate.

Climb the single wooden stile to cross a short, grassy field to a gate and track. Immediately turn left off the track on to a path that is bound either side by a tall hedge. At Upper Green Farm turn right along the access road to Upper Green Place. At the road turn left, walking into Great Bowden village.

In 100 metres turn right through a broken gate just before the red pillar box. A well-used path takes you to a wooden kissing gate and access to a wider path. After the next wooden kissing gate, cross a dyke to reach a junction of paths. Bear right and begin the ascent of the highest hill on the walk. At the top of the hill do admire the view behind before continuing past a pond and through the kissing gate. A path now heads for a modern housing estate where another wooden kissing gate allows entry into an alleyway.

Turn left along The Ridgeway as far as Great Bowden Road. Turn right along this road, passing some pretty houses which have interesting names. Pause to inspect the defunct church of St Mary in Arden, Market Harborough, which has been retained as a monument of special interest to the locality. If you wish to look around the interior of the ruins the key can be obtained on request from the Council Offices in Market Harborough. Remarkably, many of the headstones in the churchyard date back to 1775 or earlier.

At the road junction, turn right towards the town centre along St Mary's Road. After 400 metres the church of St Dionysius will be found and you need to turn right on to High Street. At the next side road, turn right, then left on to Church Street to return to the Coffee Shop.

Walk 12. Stanford Hall, Lutterworth

Route: Stanford on Avon – River Avon – Swinford – The Rookery – Stanford on Avon – Stanford Hall.

Start: St Nicholas's church, Stanford on Avon. GR 589788

Distance: 4¼ miles

Maps: OS Landranger 140 Leicester and Coventry area and OS Pathfinder 956 Rugby.

Terrain: Flat walking across mainly grassy fields. Small amount of road walking by Stanford Hall.

Public Transport: None

By Car: From M1 Junction 20 or A427 follow brown signs for Stanford Hall along minor roads to Stanford on Avon. Limited parking around the church in the village.

The Tea Shop

The Stables Tea Room at Stanford Hall has been open since 1958, the same length of time as the hall. The present proprietors, Marianne and Michael Clarke, have been in charge since 1991. Converted from the old stables, the tea room is located upstairs in the former servants' quarters. There is seating for 100 people in two rooms, with a side room downstairs where dogs and their owners can also enjoy refreshments, well away from the main food area.

Home-made afternoon teas, cream teas, cakes and scones are normally available, while on special event days breakfasts, light lunches and snacks are also served. If you are looking for a light lunch do try the Roast Ham Salad, it is delicious.

One point to bear in mind is that the tea rooms can only be reached by entrance to the grounds. There is an admission charge to the grounds in the region of £2 per person, but it is well worth it. In fact, some motorists from the nearby M1 call at the tea rooms for lunch or tea. Having paid the entrance fee and cost of the meal, it is still cheaper than stopping at the service station on the motorway and the food is better!

Opening Hours: 14.00 – 17.30 – Saturdays, Sundays, bank holiday Mondays and the following Tuesdays. 9.00 – 17.30 Event Days (list available from the hall). Open Easter Saturday to the end of September. Telephone 01788 860250

Stanford Hall

The hall is four miles from Lutterworth, located in the most southwestern part of Leicestershire. The county border with Northamptonshire at this point is the River Avon, which flows gently through the park at Stanford. Standing near the central crossroads of England, Stanford Hall was built in 1697 for Sir Roger Cave and is still home to his descendants.

This superb building has a lofty ballroom, grandly resplendent in pink and gold with its painted ceiling and renowned collection of Stuart pictures and relics. There is a mellow, panelled library lined with well over 5000 books, and the grand staircase winds past portraits of the family to bedrooms with four posters and tapestries. Family costumes are on display dating from Queen Elizabeth I's reign, including splendid embroidered waistcoats.

Percy Pilcher, England's pioneer aviator, was killed at Stanford in 1899. He crashed in the grounds while flying The Hawk. A full size replica of his 1898 flying machine is on display in the stables. Also in the stables is the Motorcycle Museum, which houses an outstanding collection of racing and vintage motorcycles, all in good working order. There is a charge to enter the museum.

If you still have time and energy for more then you can take in the walled rose garden, Old Forge and Craft Centre, a nature trail around the lake and the beautiful 14th-century church on the edge of the estate in the village. There are interesting family monuments and stained glass windows to discover. The hall is open 14.30 – 17.30 Easter Saturday to the end of September, Saturdays, Sundays, bank holiday Mondays and the following Tuesdays. The grounds open at 12 noon on event days and bank holidays but earlier, at the discretion of the owners, if the weather is very good. Telephone 01788 860250 for details.

A former estate cottage in Stanford on Avon

Swinford

An interesting village clustered around the church and public house. All Saints' Church dates to the 13th century, although parts were rebuilt in 1778 then remodelled in 1895. The Chequers pub is about 400 years old and was converted from three cottages that belonged to Stanford Estate. At one time it was a coaching inn with stables at the rear that are still visible. In bygone days beer was brewed for the estate and an oast house made up part of the stable block.

The Route

Start from St Nicholas's Church, Stanford on Avon, located in the village centre at the crossroads. Walk along the road to Cold Ashby, noting Stanford House hidden away in the impressive gardens. As you walk out of the village, notice three former estate cottages which were built in 1929 with beautiful thatched roofs. Built as tied cottages for the workers at Stanford Hall, they are now private residences.

Just past the Willows Country Club, turn right at a bridleway signpost for Lilbourne. Pass through the wooden gate on to a grassy field path which runs alongside the old railway line. In fact, the old station building has been converted into the country club. Continue ahead through several gates, following the black waymarker arrows and heading all the time for the A14. Upon reaching a bridleway signpost alongside the A14, do not cross but continue for a further 100 metres to a public footpath signpost.

To the right of the post is a small, wooden gate in the corner of the field. Walk across the field diagonally, heading for the church at Swinford in the distance. Still quite close to the very busy A14, cross the footbridge over the River Avon with a wooden stile at each end. Go diagonally left for 50 metres to another wooden footbridge across a ditch. Cross then turn right on to a farmer's track, walking next to a tall hedge. A line of new stiles, by the boundary hedge, need to be climbed as you take the obvious path to Swinford. A large, wooden farm gate and small stile allow you to join the road into Swinford village.

As you walk into the village you will notice a row of cottages which were built in 1881. At the road junction turn right on to High Street, passing the Chequers public house. Follow the B5414 through the village then where the road bends sharply to the right, locate a stone stepping stile and public footpath signpost hidden in the hedge.

A path crosses the playing fields to a row of trees, where you continue alongside a hedge to a stone stile in the left-hand corner of the field. Cross the next field, making for an electricity transmission pylon ahead. Just before the pylon, cross a footbridge then continue over the field slightly to the left. Climb two stiles either side of a ditch then continue to the left of a large wood called The Rookery.

Pass through a metal farm gate, still alongside the wood, to come to a stile and old metal gate. Climb and turn right on to a track. Follow it for 250 metres to the road. Turn right and walk along the quiet road, now for the first time glimpsing Stanford Hall across the parkland. Cross the road bridge over the River Avon then follow along the road for a further quarter mile to return to Stanford on Avon and the starting point by the church.

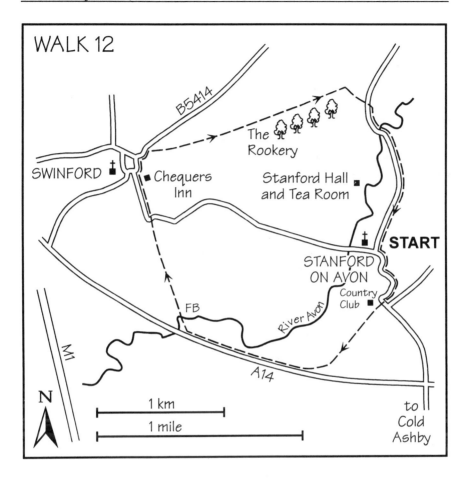

WALK 12

B5414

The Rookery

SWINFORD

Chequers Inn

Stanford Hall and Tea Room

START

STANFORD ON AVON

Country Club

FB

River Avon

M1

A14

N

1 km

1 mile

to Cold Ashby

Walk 13. Tilton on the Hill

Route: Tilton on the Hill – Colborough Hill – Stone Lodge Farm – Halstead House Farm Tea Room – Halstead – Tilton on the Hill.

Start: St Peter's Church, Tilton on the Hill. GR 743056

Distance: 4¼ miles

Maps: OS Landranger 141 Kettering, Corby and surrounding area and OS Pathfinder 895 Leicester (East) and Houghton on the Hill.

Terrain: Undulating countryside with several climbs. Well-waymarked paths and tracks. A section of walking along a gated road.

Public Transport: Very infrequent bus services from Leicester and Melton Mowbray to Tilton on the Hill, operated by A& S Travel and Ausden Clarke respectively.

By Car: Tilton on the Hill can be reached by the A47 Leicester to Peterborough road, turning on to the B6047 Melton Mowbray to Market Harborough road. Parking is available along Melton Road or at the Rose and Crown public house. Please ask permission first.

The Tea Shop

Halstead House Farm Tea Room is part of a working farm, and is well signposted from Tilton on the Hill. The farm is, in fact, situated in Halstead, about half a mile to the east of Tilton on the Hill. John and Susan Driver opened the tea room in 1985, having converted a 200-year-old farm building which was used previously as a bottling room for a retail milk round. In another part of the old building there was a baker's oven and copper boiler. During the Second World War the land girls had a bathroom in the building.

The tea room offers a fine array of home-made cakes, jams and, together with the traditional cream teas. Light lunches are also served and the tea room is licensed for alcoholic beverages. Food and drink can be enjoyed in the large garden of the house close to the lake. If the weather is wet, don't worry, there is plenty of room as the party room is opened in The Quail Shed. Do take a leisurely stroll through

Old horse-drawn hay and muck cart, Halstead House Farm

the garden after taking tea, and drink in the plethora of colourful flowers in this idyllic setting.

Opening Hours: Easter to early October – weekdays 12 noon – 17.30, weekends 10.00 – 17.30. Closed Mondays except bank holidays. Telephone 0116 259 7239

Halstead House Farm and Nature Trail

Halstead House Farm is a working farm producing over 20 000 turkeys per year. The farm trail gives an ideal chance to walk amongst pigs, goats, rabbits and various breeds of poultry, all living in their favoured environment. Out in the undulating fields are rare breeds of cattle, sheep, goats and donkeys. The farm has been open since 1994 and other attractions include a museum, nature trail and farm shop. The farm and nature trail is open Easter to early October, 10.00 – 17.30. Closed Mondays except bank holidays.

Halstead

Now recognised as part of Tilton on the Hill, the small village still manages to retain its own identity. Halstead Grange dates to 1844, with the cellar originally used for making Stilton cheese. Halstead House was built in the late 18th century and was formerly the home of the Lords of the Manor of Halstead. The house is part of the farm and can only be viewed from its exterior.

Tilton on the Hill

At 700 feet (213m) above sea level, Tilton on the Hill is the highest village in Leicestershire and Rutland. From its elevated position the views are extremely fine and extensive. It is extremely popular with walkers as many footpaths radiate from the village.

The village dates back to possibly the Bronze Age, with its name being derived from the Anglo-Saxon Tila's tun (Tila's settlement). From medieval times until the 17th century the landowners were the Digby family. The most famous was Everard Digby who, in 1603, was knighted by James I at Belvoir Castle. Two years later he was to lose his life as he was found to be involved in the Gunpowder Plot.

St Peter's Church is the highest landmark in the village. Built at the end of the 12th century, this ironstone church with its tapering steeple has a wealth of stone gargoyles. One of the features of the churchyard is the avenue of cherry trees – so pretty in summer. Another fine building in the village is the Rose and Crown public house. Dating from 1707, it is thought that an earlier timber-framed building stood here as the pub contains timber posts at its core.

Whatborough Hill

At 755 feet (230m), this is the highest point in Harborough District. It is said that when the wind blows straight from Siberia it can be felt on top of the hill. Little wonder that the early village of Whatborough which stood on the slopes of the hill was deserted by 1494!

The Route

St Peter's Church is located in the centre of the village by the crossroads. Join Main Street and walk past the entrance to the church, following the road round to reach another crossroads at the south of the village. Turn left along Loddington Road, admiring many of the stone cottages on both sides of the road. Ignore the Midshires Way

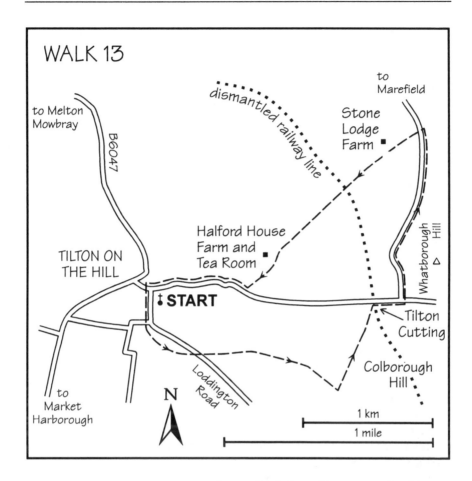

WALK 13

to Melton Mowbray

B6047

to Marefield

dismantled railway line

Stone Lodge Farm ■

TILTON ON THE HILL

Halford House Farm and Tea Room ■

Whatborough Hill △

‡ START

Tilton Cutting

to Market Harborough

N

Loddington Road

Colborough Hill

1 km

1 mile

public bridleway signpost at the end of the village, continuing on past a public footpath signpost to Halstead to reach another footpath signpost on the left.

Pass through the metal gate and walk ahead in the direction of the yellow waymarker arrow, climbing a small hill to a yellow-topped waymarker post. Continue over the next field as shown, enjoying the long view to a metal farm gate. Bear slightly to the right across the grassy field to locate a stile and market post in the far left-hand corner of the field. An obvious path now takes you over an arable field, bringing you to a track.

Turn left on to the track and follow uphill to a metal gate. Continue ahead, now noting Whatborough Hill in the distance. The path canters downhill to a new wooden gate and a road. Turn right along this road, crossing over the old LNWR/GNR joint railway line that linked Market Harborough to Melton Mowbray. From the road bridge a short detour could be made into Tilton Cutting, which is a nature reserve managed by the Leicestershire and Rutland Trust for Nature Conservation. In a further 200 metres turn left on to a gated road for Marefield.

This very quiet road takes you alongside Whatborough Hill and needs to be walked for three-quarters of a mile, as far as the second access drive to Stone Lodge Farm where a public footpath signpost will be found. Turn left, climb the stile, then go downhill to a wooden stile to the left of the farm and buildings. Aim for the next stile, sandwiched between two gates, then descend to the old railway track. An awkward climb up the embankment brings you on to the old trackbed. Cross as shown and rejoin the field path that leads back uphill to a pair of yellow-topped waymarker posts either side of a hedge.

Follow the field path around to the left alongside a hedge to the next yellow-topped waymarker post. Here, continue ahead, but now walking along a field track to Halstead House Farm. Join the farm trail briefly to pass the display of ancient farm implements, stopping perhaps to examine the particularly fine example of a horse-drawn hay and muck cart. Turn left at the end of the farm buildings on to a surfaced lane where the official entrance to the farm is found. Here the tea room will be located and tickets can be purchased to the farm trail and museum.

To continue with the walk, rejoin the lane passing Halstead House that leads to the road. Turn right towards Tilton on the Hill, following the road for half a mile to return to the church.

```
┌─────────────────────────────────────────────────┐
│  ┌───────────────────────────────────────────┐  │
│  │          Walk 14. Billesdon               │  │
│  └───────────────────────────────────────────┘  │
└─────────────────────────────────────────────────┘
```

Route: Billesdon – Billesdon Coplow – Sludge Hall – Sludge Hall Hill – Seldom Seen Farm Tea Room – Billesdon.

Start: The War Memorial, Billesdon. GR 719028

Distance: 6 miles

Maps: OS Landranger 141 Kettering, Corby and surrounding area and OS Pathfinder 895 Leicester (East) and Houghton on the Hill.

Terrain: Undulating countryside with clear paths and bridleways. Steep climb from Sludge Hall with glorious views. Small amount of quiet, minor road walking.

Public Transport: Leicester to Peterborough 747 service runs every two hours during the day via Billesdon (operated by Midland Fox). Limited Sunday service.

By Car: Billesdon is eight miles from Leicester, just off the A47 Leicester to Uppingham road. There is plenty of parking in the village, especially around the green at The Market Place.

The Tea Shop

Seldom Seen Farm Tea Room has been operating since 1975 and is an integral part of the pick-your-own fruit farm. The tea room and farm is run by Robert and Claire Symington, with Claire taking responsibility for the baking of a delicious assortment of home-made cakes and biscuits as well as cream teas. Claire is a trained chef and caterer who formerly worked with the Prue Leith organisation. What the tea room offers is good, down to earth food with prices to match. The actual tea room is very small, seating 18 maximum inside, but many outside at the picnic tables. The views across the countryside are fantastic and although the internal surroundings are basic, the panoramic view more than compensates.

This is a very popular location for picking your own fruit so be warned, the tea room is also extremely busy with pickers developing a thirst after toiling in the fields. Do try a cream tea for under £1.50.

You will get a pot of tea with a home-made scone, jam and fresh cream. Excellent value and superb food!

Opening Hours: 11.00 – 18.00 daily throughout the fruit picking season (second week of June to end of August). Telephone 0116 259 6742

Seldom Seen Farm

Seldom Seen Farm is a mixed farm of grassland and arable with a large area for fruit picking. The 700 feet contour line runs through the farm, giving spectacular views far and wide. In 1975 fruit picking was introduced with pick-your-own strawberries available. Since that date this market has expanded and today nine different varieties of fruit may be picked in season. There is a farm shop which sells a wide range of local produce, jams made from the fruit, chutney, honey, potatoes and broad beans. In December a Christmas Farm Shop has poultry, Christmas trees, home baking and home-grown frozen fruit and vegetables for sale.

Seldom Seen Farm Tea Room is only open during the fruit picking season

Billesdon

A large village located eight miles from Leicester and now bypassed by the busy A47 Leicester to Uppingham road. Set within beautiful rolling countryside, Billesdon has existed for over 1000 years as an agricultural community. Its name means 'Bills' Hill' and was given by the early Anglo-Saxon settlers to the large hill nearby, today known as Billesdon Coplow. In the Domesday Book the village name was recorded as 'Billesdone'.

In 1618 Billesdon was granted a weekly Friday market together with two annual fairs, but all have been discontinued long ago. At the centre of the village is the green where a fine market cross, dating to the 14th century, and war memorial stand. This area is known as the Market Place and there are many fine old buildings in the vicinity. At the end of Church Street is the church of St John the Baptist, built in the 13th century on the site of an earlier building. The churchyard contains a grand collection of Swithland Slate tombstones, whilst just beneath the clock the numerals of a previous clock face can be seen. This is the oldest part of the village and also the prettiest. There are many beautiful cottages around the church, and the adjacent schoolroom of 1650 and former vicarage must be inspected.

Billesdon Coplow

Just over one mile from the village is Billesdon Coplow, a distinctive hill covered in trees. The word 'coplow' means 'the summit' and 'mound', and it is probably a burial mound. In 1790 Coplow House was built with an eye-catching, white stucco front. In those days the house could be seen from Kibworth as fewer trees surrounded the building. To the east of Coplow lies Life Hill where Roman remains have been found. Small quarries here at one time produced the stone for the village buildings and the church extension.

The Route

Begin the walk from the war memorial on the village green in the centre of Billesdon. Walk along Leicester Road, passing the White Hart public house, as far as Coplow Lane. Turn right on to the lane then in 75 metres turn left at a public footpath signpost. An enclosed grassy path leads to a stile and a yellow-topped waymarker post. Follow the field perimeter path as shown by the arrow, keeping close to a hedge. Continue ahead downhill at the next waymarker post to reach the busy A47 Leicester to Uppingham Road.

Cross to the public footpath signpost opposite then descend a steep bank to a stile below. Go over a grassy field to a stile and continue on, now making for the large wooded hill of Billesdon Coplow ahead. Cross a one-hand footbridge over Coplow Brook then aim for a hedge opposite. The path is fairly obvious and well waymarked across the fields.

At Home Farm pass through two farm gates in quick succession, passing through the farmyard as directed. Join the access drive for Billesdon Coplow House, ignoring the turn to the house to reach a minor road. Turn right along the road towards Tilton on the Hill, walking by Billesdon Coplow Wood for a quarter of a mile to a road junction. Turn left towards Keyham, but in 100 metres turn right at a public bridleway signpost to Cold Newton Lodge.

Leave the track at a metal gate to join a field path which runs alongside the track. Just before the end of the field, turn right through a wooden gate and back on to the track. Continue for 200 metres to a small swing gate. Follow the field perimeter path around the rear of the house at Cold Newton Lodge. Go through a pair of wooden gates that allow you to join a wide field path alongside a hedge ahead. Do not turn left at this junction of bridleways. Turn right through a small gate in the hedge and cross the next field diagonally to Cold Newton Grange. A sign above the door of the house states that the building was erected in 1774.

Pass through an old farm gate then cross a farm track, making for a small gate which is inset ahead. Once through the gate, turn left, down to the bottom of the field to locate an old stile. Turn right along a grassy track that leads you to a wooden gate, then right again, on to Enderbys Lane. Walk along the quiet road for 275 metres to a public footpath signpost next to the entrance to Sludge Hall. Go through two gates either side of the access drive to the hall.

A steep hill climb takes you up Sludge Hall Hill, where from the top there are many lovely, panoramic views to drink in. On the skyline Ratcliffe Power Station and the television mast at Waltham can be seen while closer to hand is Quenby Hall and the church at Cold Newton. Head for a small copse ahead from the hilltop, then walk along the left-hand side of the copse to locate a stile in the wire fence.

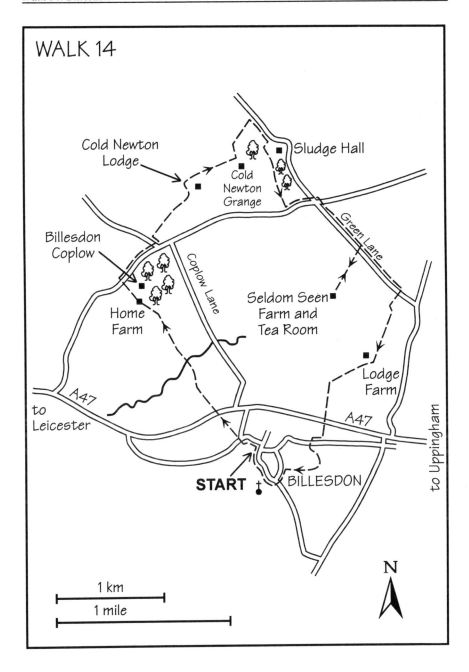

WALK 14

Climb and walk past the children's play area, across a grassy field to a wooden swing gate and the road. Turn left and walk along the road to the crossroads, turning right towards Skeffington on Green Lane.

The minor road is extremely quiet to walk along and there are further fine views to enjoy. After a quarter of a mile the entrance to Seldom Seen Farm is reached, and hopefully by now you will have worked up an appetite to enjoy Mrs Symington's cream teas or home-made cakes. The walk continues along the road for a further quarter mile in the same direction to a public bridleway signpost on the right. Follow the field perimeter path close to a hedge to a large hedge gap. Pass through and turn left on to the next field path to a new, small, wooden gate. Cross the next field and continue alongside the boundary hedge to a large, wooden gate by Lodge Farm.

Cross two access roads to a hedge gap then turn right along the field perimeter path by the farm as shown by a blue waymarker arrow. Follow around the field, adjacent to a boundary wire fence, and pass through two gates fairly close together. Continue to the brow of the next field where you find an obvious farmer's track. Turn left along the green track that leads you to the busy A47 again. Cross to the public bridleway signpost opposite to rejoin the field path. At the bottom of the lush, green field, pass through the gate on to the road, turn right into Billesdon.

Walk along the road for 100 metres to the entrance to the cemetery. Turn left on to an obvious field path that is slightly raised. Follow the route of the waymarker posts over several fields to come to Brook Lane in Billesdon. Turn left, then right past the church of St John the Baptist, continuing through the village to the war memorial on the green.

Walk 15. Stonton Wyville

Route: Stonton Wyville – Tur Langton – Church Langton – Stonton Road – Mill Farm Tea Rooms – Stonton Wyville.

Start: St Denis Church, Stonton Wyville. GR 736951

Distance: 4 miles

Maps: OS Landranger 141 Kettering, Corby and surrounding area and OS Pathfinder 916 Wigston and Kibworth Beauchamp.

Terrain: Beautiful, undulating countryside. Well-defined field footpaths with the odd climb. Small amount of very quiet road walking.

Public Transport: None worthy of note

By Car: Stonton Wyville is seven miles from Market Harborough town centre. Use the B6047 from Harborough to Church Langton. Stonton Wyville is then signposted along minor roads.

The Tea Shop

Mill Farm Tea Rooms, Stonton Wyville are run by Bill and Diana Sanderson and opened in 1993. The tea rooms open just at weekends and bank holidays as Bill has the farm to run in the week while Diana also works. The tea rooms are contained within the farmhouse, with two rooms which used to house mill machinery having been converted especially for this purpose. 36 people can be seated with additional seating available outside on the lawn.

Afternoon teas are their speciality but they are also open for morning coffee and light lunches. A good range of snacks, sandwiches and home-made cakes are available while a 'specials' board gives details of seasonal dishes that must be tried. Recommended is the fresh salmon with a herb crust, mango salsa and salad. If feeling hungry, why not try the Sanderson special – a selection of sandwiches, savouries, scones with jam and cream, dainty cakes and a pot of tea? As you enjoy your tea, do take in the original surroundings of the stone-flagged floor and the whitewashed stone walls. Farming implements decorate the walls, and old implements are being dredged up all the time to add to the display. If feeling tired after the walk, don't worry, you are welcome to stay for bed and breakfast!

Opening Hours: 11.00 – 18.00 Saturdays, Sundays and bank holidays (open March – end of October). Telephone 01858 545301

Mill Farm

Mill Farm is located on the left-hand side of the road from Tur Langton as you approach Stonton Wyville. The Sanderson family have lived here and worked at Mill Farm since 1912 but the farmhouse is considerably older, dating to the 18th century. There has been a house on the site since the Domesday Book. Currently, Mill Farm is part of the Brudenell estate, with the Brudenell family having connections with the village for centuries. Mill Farm was formerly a watermill which was once known as Water Mill House. There is now no milling machinery left and it is believed that the mill ceased around 1863.

Stonton Wyville

The village was mentioned in the Domesday Book as 'Stantone'. At that time it had two mills which were valued at 5s 4d (27p), one being Water Mill House. In 1605 it was recorded that there was still more than one mill in the village. The prosperity of the village is said to have come from its milling activities and the memorial fishponds which can still be seen clearly. For some time during the medieval period the village was called Staunton Brudenell after the Brudenell family, which has had connections with the village since Henry VIII's time. There are only 10 houses, including Mill Farm, and the church in the village.

Tur Langton

Probably the most eye-catching building in Tur Langton is the church: not for its beauty but its brashness. St Andrew's church was rebuilt in red brick on a new site in 1866. It is rather out of place in this beautiful countryside. At the west end of the village there are small remains of the old church near to the 17th-century manor house.

St Peter's church, Church Langton

Church Langton

Church Langton is the largest village of the Langtons, a group of five settlements four miles north of Market Harborough. It was the first of the five settlements and has the mother church of the group. Pause by the village green by the war memorial to see the former rectory. In its time it was 'the finest rectory in England'. Built for William Hanbury, rector from 1753 to 1778, it is a fine, symmetrical, red-brick house with limestone edgings. Behind the old rectory is St Peter's Church with its fine, high tower dating back to the 13th century. William Hanbury organised great music festivals in the church between 1759 and 1763. In September 1759 Handel's *Messiah* was performed, the first time that a classical piece of music was played in a parish church.

The Route

After a brief examination of the tiny church in Stonton Wyville, walk back out of the village towards Cranoe Road. Walk for 20 metres to a public footpath signpost and yellow-topped waymarker post. Pass through a pair of wrought iron gates on to a meadow path alongside a tall hedge. The route ahead is well waymarked to a footbridge over a stream.

Cross, then make for a metal gate in the right-hand hedge. Climb the stile adjacent to the gate and walk uphill on the field perimeter path. Once over the next stile there are superb views from the top of the hill of the surrounding undulating countryside. Continue over a number of small fields, very clearly marked, to reach a line of three stiles almost touching one another. A steady climb uphill remarkably brings you to another trio of stiles, all together, and from here the spire of Tur Langton church can be seen. Climb two stiles in quick succession then join a stony track that will bring you into the village of Tur Langton.

Turn left past the Bull's Head and continue along the road out of the village to a road turning to Cranoe. On the opposite side of the road is a stile and public footpath signpost. Go diagonally along the field footpath to a yellow-topped waymarker post, passing by the rear of the red-brick church. Climb a double stile then head for the next marker post by a corner of the field and a line of trees. Go straight ahead to the right-hand of two stiles opposite in the hedge.

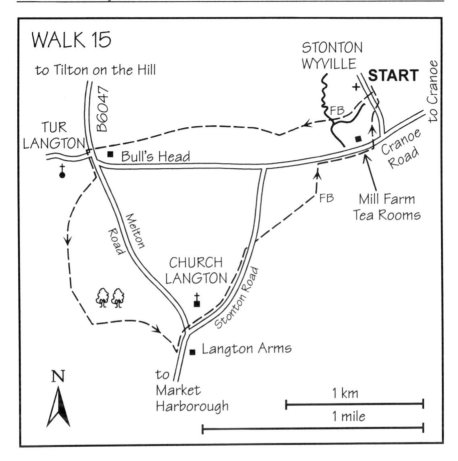

WALK 15

to Tilton on the Hill

STONTON
WYVILLE   **START**

to Cranoe

B6047

FB

TUR
LANGTON

Bull's Head

FB   Mill Farm
Tea Rooms

Cranoe
Road

Melton
Road

CHURCH
LANGTON

Stonton Road

Langton Arms

N

to
Market
Harborough

1 km

1 mile

Head downhill on the field path, as indicated by the waymarker arrows, to two yellow-topped posts close together.

At a junction of footpaths, turn left and walk uphill, passing to the right of a small wood. Cross the next field diagonally to the left, climbing two stiles close together. Head now along the field perimeter path that leads towards the magnificent church of Church Langton. An obvious path takes you over two fields then you need to bear right to the next stile. From here West Langton Hall may be glimpsed through the trees. Follow the left-hand hedge to reach a stile at the entrance drive to The Hollies farm in Church Langton.

Turn left and walk along the road into the village, passing The Langton Arms, then turn right on to Stonton Road. A pleasant walk through the village takes you past the church and school. Continue along the road, away from Church Langton, for a quarter of a mile and locate a public footpath signpost about halfway down the hill. Go through the farm gate then cross the rough, grassy field in the direction of the signpost. There is not an obvious path to follow but the next field has a defined path which brings you to a one-hand, wooden footbridge. Cross and rejoin the field perimeter path alongside a hedge to come to Cranoe Road. Turn right and walk along the road for 300 metres to the tea rooms at Mill Farm.

A warm welcome awaits at the popular tea rooms, and on a pleasant sunny day, why not enjoy a tea al fresco? Do note the large sundial on the farmhouse – its identical to the one on Stonton Wyville church. Fully refreshed, continue along the road for a further 100 metres to a public footpath signpost. A wooden swing gate gives access to a grassy field where a path leads to the village. Turn left and retrace your footsteps back to the church.

Walk 16. Newtown Linford

Route: Newtown Linford – Bradgate House Ruins – Hallgates – Cropston Leys – Swithland – Swithland Woods – Old John Folly – Newtown Linford – Jade Tearooms.

Start: Bradgate Park Country Park car park, Newtown Linford. GR 523096

Distance: 8 miles

Maps: OS Landrangers 129 Nottingham and Loughborough area and 140 Leicester and Coventry area. OS Pathfinder 874 (SK41/51) Loughborough (South).

Terrain: Undulating countryside. Good easy paths and tracks. Pretty walks through mature woodland. Quite a steep climb to the folly in Bradgate Park.

Public Transport: An infrequent daily bus service serves Newtown Linford from Leicester and Loughborough, operated by Barton Buses. No Sunday service.

By Car: Newtown Linford is reached by the B5327 from Markfield or Anstey. There is a large pay and display car park at Bradgate Park Country Park, Newtown Linford.

The Tea Shop

Jade Tearooms at Newtown Linford is housed in a Victorian building behind a pumping station. Originally built to house the workers that looked after the pumping station, it has been a tearooms since 1990. The present owners, Janine Doore and Richard Burton, took over in 1994, after training as hoteliers. They have developed the tea rooms in the Victorian style, tastefully decorated throughout with paintings of this period. A good, old-fashioned welcome awaits you.

The menu is excellent with breakfasts served till 11am every day. Freshly made sandwiches, toasties and baguettes are available all day, while from noon jacket potatoes with a choice of fillings, all served with salad garnish, may be enjoyed. Main meals are served from 12.00 to 15.00. During the colder months home-made winter warmers such as corned beef hash, steak and ale pie and fish pie are available Monday to Friday. Afternoon tea is delightful with a choice of 18 different cakes on offer each day. The cream tea is highly recommended, with a freshly baked scone filled with lashings of cream and strawberry jam and very reasonably priced. We strongly advise that you eat at the end of the walk!

Opening Hours: All year round – seven days a week. Monday to Saturday 10.00 – 18.00 (or later) in the summer. 09.00 – 17.00 (or later) – in the winter. Closed only on Christmas Day. Telephone 01530 243664.

Bradgate Country Park

The Country Park encompasses both Bradgate Park and Swithland Wood. It is the most popular country park in Leicestershire and Rutland. Bradgate Park extends to 344 hectares (850 acres) and was created 700 years ago from the Charnwood Forest as a hunting and deer park. By 1500 the park had reached its present size. Today little change has taken place, it is very much as it was then, a truly remarkable park. In 1928 Charles Bennion of Thurnby, with the help of the heirs of the Greys of Groby, purchased the park and presented it in trust for the enjoyment of the people of Leicestershire. Herds of red and fallow deer roam the bracken-covered slopes of the park and will often be found by the River Lin, which flows through the park into the adjoining Cropston Reservoir.

Bradgate House was built in 1499 by the Grey family who owned the park at that time. The house was one of the earliest unfortified country mansions in England. Lady Jane Grey was born at Bradgate in 1537 and lived much of her short life there. Following the death of her cousin, Edward VI, she was declared Queen of England on 9th July 1553. She ruled for nine days before being deposed by Mary Tudor. On 12th February 1554 Lady Jane Grey was executed at The Tower of London for treason. The ruins of the house and the chapel are open to visitors on Wednesday, Thursday, Saturday and Sunday afternoons between April and October.

Old John was built as a crenellated tower around 1784 by the 5th Earl of Stamford. The buttress on one side of it gives it the shape of a beer mug. From this familiar landmark there are fine views of the surrounding Leicestershire countryside from Bardon Hill to Billesdon Coplow.

Old John Folly, Bradgate Park

Newtown Linford

Situated at the southern entrance to Bradgate Park, the village has many fine thatched and half-timbered buildings. All Saints Church dates from the 14th century, with many additions and alterations. The most recent was in 1915 when a stained glass east window was added to commemorate the link to Lady Jane Grey. Probably the best ice cream in Leicestershire can be purchased at Eric's ice cream kiosk on Main Street.

Swithland

Swithland is very well known for its quarries, which produced roofing slates during the 18th and 19th centuries. The slate was also used for the production of headstones in church graveyards. There is a slate monument in the churchyard of the church of St Leonard as a reminder of this important bygone industry. This Charnwood Forest village consists of an extremely long main street with many magnificent stone cottages of all ages, a number of which have thatched roofs.

The Route

From the car park, go through the large, wooden kissing gate into Bradgate Park to join the tree-lined, surfaced path ahead. Alongside is the River Lin and very quickly you pass a series of stepped waterfalls. Next come the ruins of Bradgate House, where you may see or hear the peacocks that live in the grounds. A further 400 metres on from the ruins is Bradgate Country Park Visitors' Centre which tells the history of the park and Swithland Wood. Telephone 0116 2656918 for details of opening hours and admission. For the remaining walk through the park the path follows alongside Cropston Reservoir to the car park entrance at Hallgates.

Turn right at the road junction and walk for 50 metres to a public footpath signpost on your left. Climb a succession of stiles in the direction of the yellow waymarker arrows. An enclosed path brings you to a track, where you need to turn left. Walk along this track to a junction of footpaths then continue ahead through a small wood and on to a wide field path heading in the direction of the signpost for Swithland Wood.

At an obvious junction of paths turn right, ignoring the path that leads into Swithland Wood. Cross the road at Cropston Leys to a public bridleway signpost diagonally opposite. A very wide track now heads for the village of Swithland in the distance. At the end of this track pass through a wooden swing gate, staying on the track that leads to the village.

Turn left along the road, passing the Griffin Inn after 100 metres. A very pleasant walk takes you through the opulent village for three-quarters of a mile. At the last house in the village, turn left at a public footpath signpost. The track is adjacent to Woodlane Cottage, but soon narrows to a thin path between a wall and hedge. A stile allows entry into the picturesque Swithland Wood, where an obvious woodland path continues ahead.

In about 200 metres a picnic area will be found and this makes an ideal point for refreshments to be taken. This part of the wood is a magnet for birds so do look out for treecreepers, nuthatches and possibly woodpeckers. Provided you keep to the wide woodland path you will not go wrong through the wood. Pass to the left of the old quarry, which is now water-filled and fenced off for safety. Cross over a stream, continue to the end of the woodland track, then turn

WALK 16

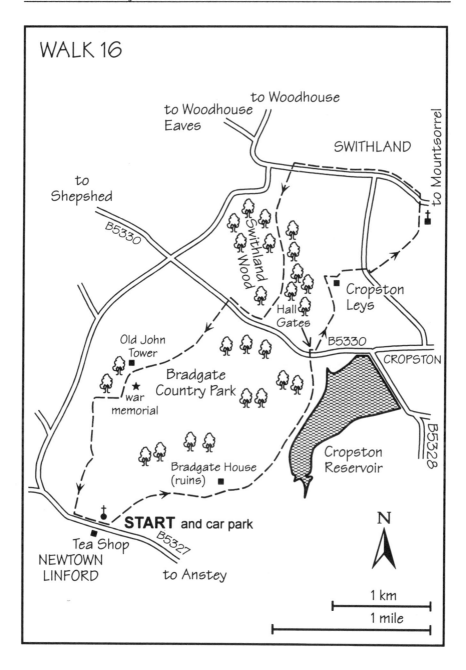

to Woodhouse

to Woodhouse
Eaves

to Woodhouse

SWITHLAND

to Mountsorrel

to
Shepshed

B5330

Swithland Wood

Cropston
Leys

Hall
Gates

Old John
Tower

B5330

CROPSTON

Bradgate
Country Park

war
memorial

Cropston
Reservoir

B5328

Bradgate House
(ruins)

START and car park

N

Tea Shop

B5327

NEWTOWN
LINFORD

to Anstey

1 km

1 mile

right on to the road that leads to the car park for the wood. Go through the car park to join a narrow woodland path that very soon crosses a stream. In a further 50 metres emerge on the B5330.

Cross to a footpath signpost to Old John and after climbing a wooden stile, join an uphill track. Go over a stile, then pass through a kissing gate that leads into Bradgate Park again. Once over the hill take one of the many paths that climb up to the folly or tower of Old John. Spend some time savouring the views from the toposcope by Old John before dropping down to the copse at the side. Walk through the copse then climb up to the war memorial for further stunning views of the park and the City of Leicester in the distance. Head now for a rocky outcrop then turn right on to a parkland path that descends to the boundary wall.

Turn left on to the path by the wall, following it ahead for a quarter of a mile to reach a narrow, wooden kissing gate set in the drystone wall. Squeeze through to join a grassy field path that wriggles its way down to the village of Newtown Linford. Turn left along the road through the village, passing the immaculate cricket ground, and in a further 100 metres Jade Tearooms will be reached. To complete the walk, turn left into the entrance of the car park next to the parish Church of All Saints.

Walk 17. Quorn

Route: Quorn and Woodhouse Station – Mill Farm – Swithland Reservoir Gardens – Great Central Railway – Woodhouse – Whatoff Lodge Farm Tea Shop – Quorn and Woodhouse Station.

Start: Quorn and Woodhouse railway station, Quorn. GR 549162

Distance: 4 miles

Maps: OS Landranger 129 Nottingham and Loughborough area and OS Pathfinder 874 Loughborough (South).

Terrain: Pleasant, easy paths alongside two streams, crossing green, open fields. A little rough track walking then a pleasant stroll through Quorn village.

Public Transport: Buses run frequently to Quorn from Leicester and Loughborough, operated by Kinch Bus and Midland Fox.

By Car: Quorn lies to the south of the A6, two miles from Loughborough. It can be approached from either Leicester or Loughborough by leaving the road at Woodthorpe roundabout and following the B591 to Woodhouse.

The Tea Shop

Whatoff Lodge Tea Shop is part of the farm buildings that lie at the end of a 400 metre farm track. Traditional farmhouse teas are prepared and served by Shirley Thomas in a converted barn which also houses the museum. A unique feature of the tea shop is the old cattle trough which runs the length of the Charnwood Forest stone building, and is now part of the seating arrangements.

The farm tea room was opened in 1987. The view of the Charnwood landscape from the whitewashed, stone building is truly remarkable. For train buffs, the Great Central Railway passes through the farm fields and you can sit enjoying a cream tea whilst watching steam trains puffing past close by. Shirley serves mainly full teas with two scones, cream and jam, and a choice of drinking tea. Cold drinks and ice cream are also sold, with everything reasonably priced. If arriving when the tea shop is about to close, don't worry, Shirley will give you a warm welcome as she is never in a hurry to lock up.

Opening Hours: 11.00 – 18.00 Tuesday to Sunday. Closed on Mondays except for bank holidays. Open from March to mid October. Telephone 01509 412127

Whatoff Lodge Farm

Whatoff Lodge is found just off Woodhouse Road in Quorn, near to the railway station. The farm comprises 101 hectares (250 acres) and is named after William Whatoff who built it in the 1830s, after the Charnwood Forest Enclosure Award of 1829. There is a farm museum which houses an interesting collection of farm implements from a bygone age. For walkers who fancy a longer walk, the farm has its own one and a quarter mile nature trail which allows you to walk amongst many varied farm animals. A useful explanatory booklet of the nature trail is available. For details of admission to the museum, farm trail and farm animals, telephone 01509 412127.

Taking tea at Whatoff Lodge tea shop, Quorn

Great Central Railway

The preserved main line railway extends for eight miles from Loughborough Central to Leicester North via Quorn and Rothley. Here is a chance to relive the experience of main line expresses in the days of steam, hauled by one or possibly two locomotives. At Loughborough Station, the locomotive shed, the sidings, signal box and museum can be seen and there are period stations at Quorn and Rothley. The line was constructed in 1894, being one of the last main lines to London to be built. Closed in 1969, attempts began to preserve something of the railway. Enormous costs meant that initially only a stretch of five and a half miles between Loughborough and Rothley was saved. In 1990, further fund raising had taken place and the line was extended to Birstall, (Leicester North). Main line steam trains run every weekend throughout the year with passenger trains on weekdays also from May to September. If you desire a ride on Britain's only main line steam railway then telephone 01509 230726 to find out more.

Quorn

Quorn, or Quorndon as it is sometimes known, is now bypassed by the modern A6. The village looks out across the Soar Valley to Barrow Upon Soar and is mainly residential, with many fine buildings. Its name is known worldwide, due to Hugo Meynell who founded the Quorn Hunt and was such a dominant figure in English foxhunting. He lived at Quorn Hall from 1753 to 1800. He did much to put Quorn on the map, generating much wealth for the village. Anyone with an interest in beautiful gardens should go along to Quorn when the annual Open Gardens event takes place. In total 53 village gardens open their gates for charity. Details are available form Loughborough TIC, telephone 01509 218113.

The Route

From Quorn and Woodhouse Station, walk along Woodhouse Road into Quorn village then turn right into Chaveney Road. Follow this road round to the left, where in a further 300 metres you will find a public footpath signpost by Mill Farm. A track takes you to a large, green gate. In 150 metres bear right through another green gate to join a pleasant, grassy path.

You now follow alongside a winding stream on a very well-used path for a quarter of a mile. There are lovely views to enjoy and you may see a steam train on the Great Central Railway line away to the right. Where the stream veers off left, look for a stile by a wooden gate. Climb and continue ahead, as before, now walking alongside a hedge. A wide field perimeter path brings you to a black, wrought iron fence belonging to the gardens of Swithland Reservoir. Follow the path around the pretty reservoir gardens then cross the iron railing footbridge over a stream. The path now heads to the railway line over a lush, green meadow. Continue next to the railway line for 250 metres to reach a stile that gives you access to a very minor road. Turn right over the bridge and in 100 metres a sign for the Leicestershire Round and a stile will be found on the right.

Join the field path, which at first follows alongside the railway line, heading in the same direction as earlier but on the opposite side of the track. Follow the path to the left, crossing a stream, then make for a solitary oak tree ahead. Climb a stile then walk by a hedge to the next stile. The well-used path bears to the left over a short field then continues next to a stream. Climb two stiles extremely close together to rejoin the field path still adjacent to the stream. Pass through a white gate by a bridleway signpost to Swithland and turn right on to a farm lane.

With Rushey Fields Farm behind, walk along the surfaced access lane, savouring the views all around. Beaumanor Hall, which was built in the 1840s for the Herrick family, stands grandly away to your left as you head along this lane. Go through a large, white gate by a pretty, stone cottage to reach a junction of lanes. Ignore the lane to Woodhouse and continue on towards the Well House.

At the next junction of tracks, turn left, still heading for the Well House. Ignore the track that goes off to the Well House, now walking along a field track that brings you to a junction of bridleways. Continue ahead for a further 100 metres, then follow around to the left, still on the track, to reach the B591.

Turn right along the road for a quarter of a mile to reach the access drive to Whatoff Lodge Farm. After enjoying a pleasant call at the tea shop and farm, continue along the road for a further 200 metres to reach the railway bridge at Quorn and Woodhouse Station.

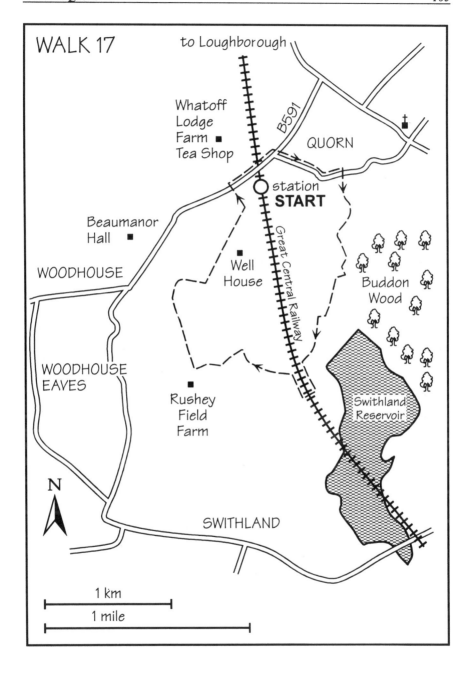

WALK 17

to Loughborough

Whatoff
Lodge
Farm ■
Tea Shop

B591

QUORN

station
START

Beaumanor
Hall ■

WOODHOUSE

Well
House ■

Great Central Railway

Buddon
Wood

WOODHOUSE
EAVES

Rushey
Field
Farm ■

Swithland
Reservoir

N

SWITHLAND

1 km

1 mile

Walk 18. Mountsorrel

Route: Mountsorrel – Sileby Mill – River Soar – Mountsorrel Lock – Stonehurst Tea Shop – Mountsorrel.

Start: The Butter Market, Leicester Road, Mountsorrel. GR 583150

Distance: 2½ miles

Maps: OS Landranger 129 Nottingham and Loughborough area and OS Pathfinder 874 Loughborough (South).

Terrain: Flat walking through beautiful Charnwood countryside. Pleasant path alongside River Soar then an interesting stroll around the village.

Public Transport: A frequent bus service calls at Mountsorrel from both Leicester and Loughborough, operated by Midland Fox and Kinch Bus.

By Car: Mountsorrel is now bypassed by the A6. Use this from either Leicester or Loughborough, leaving at the appropriate exit for the village. There is free car parking at Charnwood Borough Council car park by the memorial hall.

The Tea Shop

The Farm Tea Shop is part of Stonehurst Family Farm and Museum, but can be visited without having to pay for entry into the farmyard. Greg and Marilyn Duffin opened the tea shop and the farm in 1992 and have had to extend the tea shop three times, such is its popularity. Converted from stables and a byre for cattle, the tea shop keeps its authenticity with displays of old farm implements on the walls.

Light lunches for the family or clotted cream teas are available during the day. A display cabinet offers some extremely tempting, home made cakes and scones together with tea, coffee and soft drinks. Children are especially catered for in the tea shop – they can even hold their birthday party at the farm!

Opening Hours: Daily, all year round, 10.00 – 17.00. Telephone 01509 413216.

Stonehurst Family Farm and Museum

Situated on Loughborough Road in Mountsorrel, walkers of all ages will find something to enjoy at the farm. Young walkers will want to wander amongst the small sheep, pigs, rabbits and hens, while at 'cuddle corner', depending on the time of year, lambs can be cuddled. There is an interesting farm trail and motor museum with its vintage cars, motorbikes and memorabilia on display. Do inspect the old blacksmith's shop and buy fresh produce from the farm shop. An admission charge is made to the farm attractions and motor museum, but it is well worth paying.

Mountsorrel

With the opening of the A6 bypass, Mountsorrel has returned to a quiet, peaceful village, much to the delight of its inhabitants. The village is famous for its large granite quarry which supplies granite chippings to the construction industry all over the country. Redland Aggregates have a two-mile, continuous, mechanised conveyor belt that takes these chippings to the railway ridings at Barrow on Soar, passing through the Soar Valley.

Much of the village is built of red granite quarried from a hill that once overlooked Mountsorrel. A castle used to stand on this hill, but both have long disappeared. On Leicester Road is the domed and columned Butter Market which was built in 1793. The parish church dates back to 1800 and is built of local stone.

Below Mountsorrel in the Soar Valley flows the picturesque River Soar. Here is a splendid scene with brightly-painted narrow boats and pleasure craft gliding along the water, surrounded by green meadows. The whole area is a mecca for water birds and it is not unusual to spot herons, cormorants and kingfishers on this stretch of the river.

The Route

Keeping the Butter Market on your right, walk along Leicester Road as far as a sign for The Memorial Playing Fields. Turn left by a Leicestershire Round signpost pointing to Cossington (1½ miles), passing alongside the small village hall. Follow the access road to the children's play area then pass through a colourful gate to join a path that leads into the playing fields.

Go by Mountsorrel Castle Cricket Club pavilion, making for a yellow-topped waymarker post ahead. An obvious path takes you through a new housing estate that at the time of writing was under construction. This path brings you to the high bank of the A6 bypass, where you need to turn right on to the alternative route that leads to an underpass 260 metres away. Turn left and walk through the underpass then turn left in the direction of the Leicestershire Round arrows to walk back alongside the A6 bypass to reach a stile and Leicestershire Round signpost.

Cross the field to a large, wooden stile, then cross a stream and pass through a small wood. Continue ahead over the next field to a stile, where a long, raised, concrete flood path takes you to a bridge. Cross and continue along the concrete flood path to reach the River Soar and Sileby Lock. From here there is a fine view of Sileby Boatyard where narrow boats may be hired for one day or up to a week for cruising along the river.

Turn left along the riverside path, ignoring the bridges that cross the river to the old Sileby Mill. In 200 metres a wooden, convex-shaped bridge needs to be crossed to continue on the riverside path, now on the opposite bank. As you progress along the river there are extremely pretty views to enjoy of the open countryside that makes

Crossing the River Soar at Sileby Mill

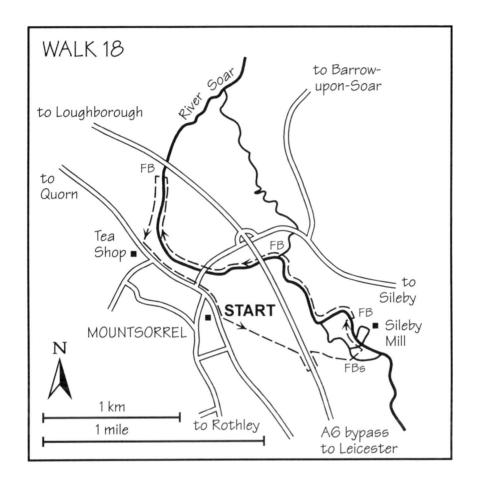

WALK 18

to Loughborough

River Soar

to Barrow-upon-Soar

to Quorn

FB

Tea Shop ■

FB

■ START

MOUNTSORREL

to Sileby

FB

■ Sileby Mill

N

FBs

1 km

1 mile

to Rothley

A6 bypass to Leicester

this part of the Soar Valley so desirable. A number of easy stiles are crossed before a narrow bridge by a weir is encountered. Cross this bridge carefully, then climb two stiles in quick succession before passing beneath the bridge for the A6 bypass again.

A very pleasant, grassy field path now leads to Mountsorrel Lock where the Waterside Inn, which was established in 1849, will be found. You now need to cross the road bridge to rejoin the riverside path ahead. Very soon you will go under a brick-built bridge that dates to 1860, and if you look up you may be able to see the conveyor belt taking stone chippings down to the railway sidings from the quarry in Mountsorrel.

About 200 metres further on, climb the bridge over the River Soar and turn back on yourself to a wooden stile in 50 metres. Climb two stiles then join a gravelled track that passes alongside a small caravan site. At the road, turn left on to Loughborough Road and in 100 metres Stonehurst Family Farm and Museum will be found. After calling at the farm, it is a matter of continuing along the road through Mountsorrel village to complete the walk by returning to the Butter Market.

Walk 19. Wartnaby

Route: Wartnaby – Saxelbye Pastures – Grimston – Old Dalby Wood – Old Dalby – Marriott's Spinney – Stonepits Farm Tea Room – Wartnaby.

Start: The Information Board, Wartnaby. This is found just past the church at the village road junction. GR 712231

Distance: 6 miles

Maps: OS Landranger 129 Nottingham and Loughborough area and OS Pathfinder 854 Scalford and Nether Broughton.

Terrain: Very well-waymarked paths and tracks. Undulating countryside with many good views. No road walking except through villages.

Public Transport: An infrequent daily service from Melton Mowbray to Bingham calls at Wartnaby, operated by Barton Buses. There is no Sunday service.

By Car: Wartnaby is four miles north-west of Melton Mowbray. It may be reached by using the A606 Nottingham to Melton Mowbray road or the A46 Leicester to Newark road. Take the Salt Way, an old Roman road, which links both of these routes between Six Hills and north of Ab Kettleby. Park on the road in Wartnaby without causing an obstruction.

The Tea Shop

Stonepits Farm Tea Rooms and Licensed Restaurant is located on The Salt Way, half a mile north-west of Wartnaby village. Opened Easter 1993, the tea rooms consist of three rooms, the long room, the old kitchen and the snooker room. The building was originally a semi-detached, single storey worker's cottage for the labourers who dug the stone out of nearby pits. The upstairs was added in the early 1800s.

Janice Musson, proprietor, offers a warm welcome, old-fashioned service and a superb choice of home-cooked food from cream teas to Sunday roasts. The menu also features traditional Leicestershire fare, such as local Stilton cheese and Dickinson and Morris pork pies. There are no restrictions on the timing of the meals. You are welcome to order a pot of tea at lunch time, a full breakfast at tea time or steak and kidney pie for elevenses! Do try a salad at Stonepits Farm, salad days last all year round. Many different ingredients are used, with much of the summer lettuce and herbs grown on the farm. Very reasonably priced, the home-cooked ham salad is particularly recommended as the ham is dry-cured by a local butcher to an old recipe which he won't divulge then cooked on the farm. Bring a large container with you as ham, large, free-range eggs and steak and kidney pies (family-sized) can be purchased to take away.

Opening Hours: 11.00 – 18.00 Tuesday – Sunday (inclusive). Closed on Mondays except bank holidays. Telephone 01664 823302

Wartnaby

A very picturesque, small hamlet, some four miles north-west of Melton Mowbray, set in the beautiful North Leicestershire Wolds. The village was mentioned in the Domesday Book and its high position on the escarpment made it an important lookout point many centuries ago. In fact, the name of Wartnaby comes from an old English translation of 'watch-hill'. The hamlet is a joy to walk around,

Sheep and lambs in a paddock on the Wartnaby Estate

especially in early summer when the colours of the countryside are at their finest. Do look at St Michael's church and its 13th-century saddleback west tower, font and medieval benches.

Grimston

Grimston is a small village (population 147) surrounded by gently rolling countryside. The main part of the village is the village green where agriculture is the backbone of community life. A set of ancient stocks are found on the village green and there is a boulder stone beneath a mature chestnut tree. The parish church of St John dates to the 13th century, and when viewed on a sunny day the mellow ironstone of the exterior is extremely pleasing to the eye. This is horse country, where important racehorse stabling and training takes place. It may be that on your travels around Grimston you will see a future Grand National winner exercising along the village lanes.

Old Dalby

Located eight miles to the north-west of Melton Mowbray, it is beautifully situated below the escarpment of the North Leicestershire Wolds, The real name of the village is Wold Dalby or Dalby on the Wolds. Old Dalby Hall and the surrounding land was once owned by the Knights Hospitalier of the order of St John of Jerusalem. It has also been owned by a number of famous figures including Oliver Cromwell, 'Hanging' Judge Jeffreys and the Duke of Buckingham. Until the 1930s the hall had a squire and a full complement of staff. Today the hall is a private residence and the stables have been converted into a nursing home. The lake which is passed on the walk belongs to the hall and day tickets for fishing are available.

Old Dalby Test Track

The British Railways Board owns the test track between Melton Junction and Edwalton, a distance of 13 miles. The track is the former down line of the closed Midland Railway route between Nottingham and St Pancras via Melton Mowbray. The Research Department, which is based at Derby, has used the Old Dalby test track since the 1970s to test trains and equipment at high speed, including the ill-fated APT-E train with its unique tilt facility. The line's claim to fame occurred on 17th July 1984 when it made world headlines with the staging of a nuclear flask collision on behalf of the CEGB. In front of the media, a collision was staged at Old Dalby between a withdrawn locomotive and a flask – in order to dispel public fears of the dangers of a flask involved in a collision. The diesel locomotive ploughed into a pre-positioned nuclear flask at almost 100 mph, destroying the locomotive but leaving the flask intact.

The Route

In the heart of the village, about 200 metres from the path that goes to the church, is the information board. Leaving the board on the corner of a small green, walk up Main Street as far as a red telephone box. A public bridleway signpost shows the way along the driveway through the Wartnaby Estate – follow it for 100 metres to a large, wooden gate.

Join the track that now leads ahead, following it round to the right and passing through a large, metal gate. Continue on through two more gates before the track drops down to a yellow-topped waymarker post by a stream. A blue arrow marks the way ahead for the next half mile – the track becomes rough in places.

Cross a minor road to a large, wooden gate by a public bridleway signpost, which may be broken. A grassy field path runs downhill alongside a boundary fence, heading for the left-hand side of Saxelbye Wood. Make for a yellow-topped waymarker post that indicates where a stream is to be crossed then you need to go uphill, slightly to the right, to a fairly new swing gate. Here, join a track for 200 metres – as far as the farmhouse of Barn Farm. Go through a wooden swing gate on to a grassy path and cross the railway test track, which passes through the tunnel beneath the hill. Cross a stream then go uphill alongside a hedge, heading for a farm. A number of farm gates allow access, and after passing the sheep pens, a final farm gate at Lilac Farm brings you to the road in Grimston village.

Turn right along the road into the village, passing the village pump and church to a public footpath signpost at Red House Farm. Pass between two buildings to reach a stile where a home-made footpath sign directs you around the private garden. Walk ahead over a grassy paddock then climb three stiles very close together. Turn left to a metal gate then turn right and continue ahead over a grassy field

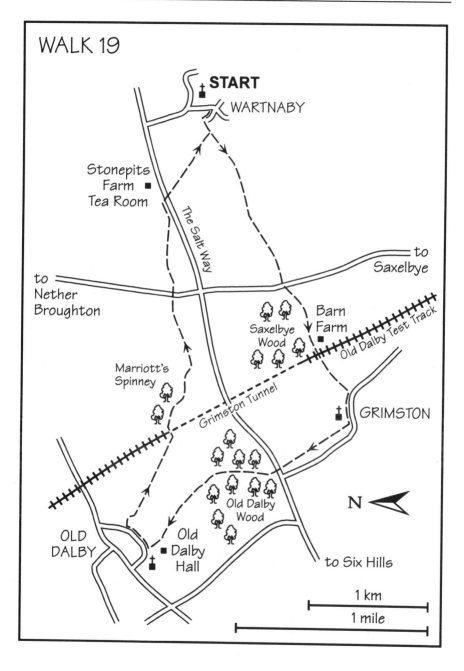

WALK 19

START
WARTNABY

Stonepits
Farm
Tea Room

The Salt Way

to
Saxelbye

to
Nether
Broughton

Saxelbye
Wood

Barn
Farm

Old Dalby Test Track

Marriott's
Spinney

Grimston Tunnel

GRIMSTON

Old Dalby
Wood

N

OLD
DALBY

Old
Dalby
Hall

to Six Hills

1 km

1 mile

alongside a hedge. A stile leads you out on to The Salt Way, an old Roman road. You need to cross to a public footpath signpost opposite for Old Dalby.

A very pretty woodland path snakes ahead into Old Dalby Wood. At a junction of tracks bear right on to the elevated woodland path, which is well waymarked. The path descends dramatically through the wood and rejoins the wider path which was left earlier. Bear right again through an avenue of trees, as indicated, then cross a small stream by the aid of a concrete pillar. Climb a stile by a gate to leave the wood. After crossing a one-hand bridge, climb a pleasant, green hill, making for the village of Old Dalby in the distance. After climbing a stile, Fishpond Plantation is entered. This small wood is extremely beautiful, being situated beneath the escarpment of the Wolds. The wood is alive with birds and is renowned as a popular haunt for both green and lesser spotted woodpeckers. A path leads out of the wood then takes you alongside Old Dalby Hall to the village of Old Dalby.

The church is seen to the left, but you need to turn right out of the village for 200 metres to a public footpath signpost. An enclosed path brings you to a stile by Dalby Lake. Continue ahead, following the waymarker posts to a track. Ignore the path that goes to the right along the track, climbing instead a stile opposite in the hedge. Make for the left stile of two ahead, then cross a large field, going uphill to the far left-hand side by the railway test track.

From the top of the hill there is a fine panoramic view of outstanding countryside, and time should be spent enjoying the extensive views of the two counties of Leicestershire and Nottinghamshire. Cross Grimston Tunnel, the mouth of the tunnel can be seen below, picking your way through a section of gorse and blackberry bushes. After a possibly boggy piece of ground, cross over a wooden, one-hand footbridge then climb a steep hill to the top, alongside Marriott's Spinney. At a junction of footpaths continue ahead for 50 metres to another junction of footpaths. The path follows alongside a line of trees to a stile. Now follow the field perimeter path by a hedge over several fields, heading for the yellow-topped waymarker posts.

Cross a minor road then carry on as before along the field perimeter edge, enjoying the superb views of the vale. At a small pond the path cuts off diagonally over a large field and to the Salt Way again.

Turn left and continue for 150 metres to reach Stonepits Farm tea room. After a refreshing drink and perhaps a cream tea, cross the road to a public footpath signpost. Climb a fence in the left-hand hedge then make for a hedge across the field. Pass through a large gap in the hedge – unfortunately there is no obvious path to follow over the next field. Make for the farm buildings in the left-hand corner of the field and here you will find a farm track. Walk past the farm buildings to reach the track where you started the walk. Retrace your steps back through Wartnaby Estate to Wartnaby village and the information board at the road junction.

Walk 20. Melton Mowbray

Route: Chapel Street Car Park – Melton Mowbray Country Park – Jubilee Way – Scalford – Glebe Farm – Melton Mowbray – Browsers Tea Shoppe.

Start: Chapel Street car park, Melton Mowbray. GR 755194

Distance: 6¾ miles

Maps: OS Landranger 129 Nottingham and Loughborough area. OS Pathfinders 875 Melton Mowbray and Syston and 854 Scalford and Nether Broughton.

Terrain: Mainly flat walking through country park and across grassy fields. Numerous stiles but no steep climbs.

Public Transport: Good bus service between Melton Mowbray – Leicester – Loughborough and Oakham, operated by Midland Fox and other operators. Train station at Melton Mowbray on the Leicester to Peterborough line. Good hourly service connects these two cities.

By Car: Melton Mowbray may be reached by a number of main roads from different towns or cities including A46 (A607) from Leicester, A60 (A6006) Loughborough, A606 from Oakham and A607 from Grantham. Pay and display parking at Chapel Street allows up to four hours, alternatively there are longer stay car parks in the town centre.

The Tea Shop

Browsers Tea Shoppe is found at Bowley Court, off Sherrard Street, 200 metres towards the town centre from the car park. The proprietor, Sylvia Smart, has owned the business since July 1987, when Browsers opened. It was purpose-built on a derelict site, along with other interesting shops. It is a traditional tea shop with a homely atmosphere, seating up to 36 inside with a further three tables outside.

All food is home-made with the menu offering a dazzling array of hot meals including vegetarian dishes, snacks, jacket potatoes, sandwiches, rolls and toasted sandwiches. There is a scrumptious choice of gateaux and desserts, all very good value. A 'specials' board changes daily, and the winter warmer is popular on colder days, especially market days. Afternoon tea is available after 14.00

and consists of tea or coffee, choice of sandwich and scone with jam and cream. Excellent value at around £2.00. After a long walk it is heaven to plonk down at Browsers, where the service is friendly and efficient, and enjoy their hospitality at reasonable expense.

Opening Hours: 09.30 – 16.30/17.00 Monday to Saturday. Closed Sundays. Telephone 01664 410085

Melton Mowbray

In the Domesday Book Melton Mowbray is referred to as 'Medeltone', meaning 'the dwelling in the middle of a district'. It has a market dating back to 1077, one of the oldest street markets in the country. A market is held every Tuesday and Saturday, with a cattle market also held on Tuesdays. This is well worth watching, especially the local farmers at work, and you can buy anything from puppies to peacocks.

Melton Mowbray is famous, of course, for Stilton cheese and pork pies. Tuxford and Tebbutt on Thorpe End have manufactured fine Stilton and Leicester cheese for over 200 years. About one-eighth of all Stilton cheese produced here is sold in overseas markets, principally in North America. Up to 100 people are employed locally and are responsible for 17 per cent of the entire volume of Stilton produced in the UK. A specialist cheese shop on King Street sells Stilton and other fine cheeses. Dickinson and Morris of Nottingham Street are the town's traditional pork pie maker. Ye Olde Pork Pie Shoppe sells produce made at the shop, and besides pork pies the premises also bakes The Original Melton Hunt Cake. This superbly rich, quality fruit cake is made to their own patented recipe that dates from 1854. Originally supplied to nobility, clergy and gentlemen of the Melton Hunt, today the cake is sold to customers all over the world.

The town has many fine buildings, none more so than Anne of Cleves' House – a wealthy, 14th-century wool merchant's dwelling, which acquired its present name when Henry VIII presented it to his divorced wife, Anne of Cleves in the mid-16th century. Nearby is St Mary's Church. Of cathedral-like appearance, it dates from 1170 and the tower dominates the town. The church is known as the stateliest and most impressive of all Leicestershire churches. A visit to Melton Carnegie Museum is recommended – there are interesting displays on fox hunting, and the history of Stilton cheese and pork pies.

Admiring the fine church of St Egelwin The Martyr at Scalford

The Jubilee Way

Opened in 1977 to mark the Queen's Silver Jubilee, this is a 15½ mile walk, mostly over fields and through pretty woodland. It begins at the Carnegie Museum in Melton Mowbray and ends at Brewer's Grave, to the east of Woolsthorpe in Lincolnshire, where it joins the Viking Way. It has been specially waymarked with Jubilee Way symbols throughout, making it extremely easy to follow and allowing walkers to really enjoy the countryside.

Scalford

Scalford is pronounced 'Scorford' and is some four miles north of Melton Mowbray. It derives its name from a ford over Scalford Brook, which rises to the east of the village and flows south to Melton Mowbray. In 1303 the village had a fair and a weekly market. Today there is a thriving business in the making of Stilton. The church, St Egelwin the Martyr, is of ironstone and grey limestone. It is believed that St Egelwin is buried here. An old market cross can also be found here.

The Route

Walk out of the top end of Chapel Street car park and pass the United Reformed church to reach Norman Way. Turn right along the busy road, keeping to the pavement as far as Snow Hill, where you turn left. At the end of the road bear right on to a surfaced path that follows alongside a wood yard. This will bring you into Melton Country Park.

In 50 metres turn right at a public footpath signpost to join the Jubilee Way as it threads its way through the park. Walk adjacent to the old Great Northern Railway as far as the children's play area. Cross the bridge over Scalford Brook to continue out of the country park to an obvious left turning on to a track. With houses on one side, walk along the track to reach a gate that leads you back into the country park. A well-used path climbs slowly to the top of the park, where there is a tranquil scene of the lake below, which has some similarity to a map of Great Britain. Pass through an obvious hedge gap then bear to the left to make for a very large public footpath signpost by the old railway bridge. Rejoin the Jubilee Way.

Ignore the steps up on to the old railway trackbed and climb a stile either side of a ditch. Walk ahead in the direction of the way-marker arrow. Pass through a large opening into the next field, where a pleasant, grassy path runs alongside Scalford Brook. The route across the fields is very clear. To the left of Melton Spinney, go through a small, wooden gate or climb a poor stile. Cross the next short field, ignoring a track that leads into the spinney. Pass through a farm gate and, keeping faith with Scalford Brook, head for a yellow-topped waymarker post beneath the tree at the end of the bridge.

The path still follows the swift-flowing brook with the tall tower of Scalford church beckoning ahead. Cross the footbridge over the brook and continue along the field perimeter hedge, on the opposite side until reaching the next footbridge. Cross back over to rejoin the field perimeter path and go ahead to a small, picturesque glade and a concrete footbridge. Cross the brook for the last time, moving away from your companion for the previous mile to cross a field making for the old railway embankment. Climb two stiles then go beneath the bridge of the old railway line. In 50 metres leave the track by climbing a stile. Go right and walk diagonally uphill to an alleyway. This enclosed path leads into Scalford village.

Turn left through the village. In 50 metres reach a small green, then turn into South Street, noting the fine church hidden behind the houses. Immediately past a house called Fairfield, turn left at a public footpath signpost. Squeeze along the alley to an enclosed stile. Walk away from the village to the next stile then turn left over the next field making for a yellow-topped waymarker post. Cross over the bridges of two disused railway lines. The first is the former Waltham Branch mineral line, while the second is a former passenger and freight line.

Climb a stile at the end of the bridge and bear half-left to a white farmer's gate. At the top of the rise, cross the next field slightly to the right, making for the next waymarker post. Here, climb two stiles in close proximity to each other to join a grassy field perimeter path. Clamber over a ditch then a stile to continue along the field perimeter edge. Repeat the process as before, then go uphill, heading for a group of trees and climbing a stile in the hedge. Cross the field to the farm buildings at Glebe Farm. Join an access track that leads to the road.

At the road junction join Holwell Lane then turn left at a road tri-

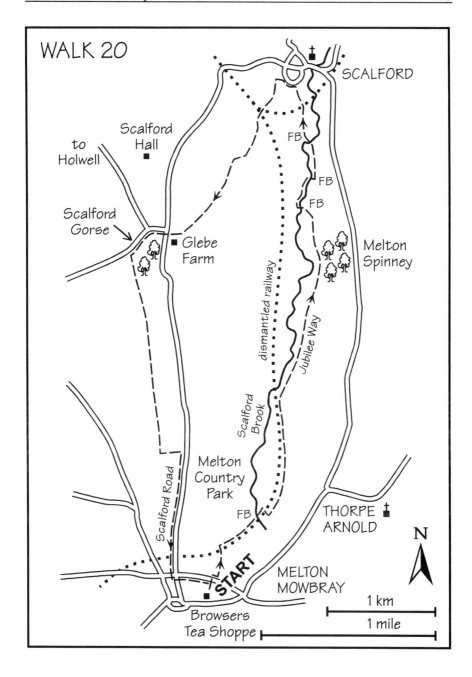

angle. Just past Scalford Gorse, turn left at a public footpath sign-post. Cross the field as shown to the next stile. As you descend over the next field, there is a panoramic view of Melton Mowbray ahead, nestling in the Wreake Valley, while over to the right is the ill-fated Asfordby Coalmine. A natural path cuts between two hills, then a raised field perimeter path brings you to a stile next to a large pair of farm gates.

Continue alongside the boundary hedge to a stile then follow alongside a deep ditch to another stile. Cross the next field to the left to a large hedge gap marked by two white posts. Head for the houses opposite then walk along an alleyway, which brings you out on to Dickens Drive. Turn left and left again into Melbray Drive to Scalford Road. Turn right, following the road back into Melton Mowbray for half a mile and passing the cattle market to reach Norman Way. Turn left then right into Chapel Street and the car park.

Walk 21. Little Dalby

Route: Hollies Farm – Little Dalby – Moscow Farm – Burrough Hill – Dalby Hills Path – Little Dalby – Hollies Farm Tea Room.

Start: Hollies Farm, Little Dalby. GR 776140

Distance: 6 miles

Maps: OS Landranger 129 Nottingham and Loughborough area and OS Pathfinder 875 Melton Mowbray and Syston.

Terrain: Green tracks and well-used paths. Some road walking. One steady climb on to Burrough Hill.

Public Transport: None

By Car: Little Dalby lies three-quarters of a mile off the A606, Melton Mowbray to Oakham road, and is four miles south-east of Melton Mowbray.

The Tea Shop

The tea room at Hollies Farm has been tastefully renovated from a building that was part of a pig farm. Opened in 1994, the tea room shares its location with a craft and antique display, both run by Mark Alton. Photographs of the conversion work decorate the wall, showing the various stages of change. Inside are four tables in the compact room, while more tables grace the courtyard and are popular in the summer.

The menu embraces tea or coffee and home-made cakes and biscuits. Although the choice is limited, the home-made cakes are mouth-watering and anyone with a sweet tooth will be delighted by the tempting display of cream cakes on offer.

Opening Hours: 11.00 – 16.30 Saturday, Sunday and bank holiday Mondays. (Closed between Christmas and Easter.) Telephone 01664 454553

Hollies Farm

The workshops at the farm have been in use since 1987 and are also run by Mark Alton. There is a furniture showroom with quality furniture on show including grandfather clocks, desks and bureaux.

Ceramics, paperweights, paintings, wooden toys, textiles and wood turning are just some the handicrafts that can be viewed in the converted buildings. The showroom is open Monday to Saturday inclusive, 09.00 – 17.00.

Little Dalby

A small hamlet hidden away in beautiful, green countryside, Little Dalby is famous for making Stilton cheese since 1720. It is argued that Mrs Orton, housekeeper at Little Dalby Hall, first produced Stilton cheese although nearby Wymondham also lays claim to making this delicious cheese before others. At the end of the walk, do take the path up the wooded hill to the isolated church of St James. The church is a listed building and was rebuilt in 1851 by the architect Brandon. Little Dalby Hall is a pale shadow of its former self. Originally the home of the Hartopps, the house was built by William Hartopp then added to over the centuries. Now much of the hall has been sold off and turned into flats.

Moscow Farm from the top of Burrough Hill

Burrough Hill

Burrough Hill stands 690 feet (210m) above sea level and is one of the highest hills around. Its summit is capped by an impressive Iron Age hill fort which dates from about 800BC. It is thought that the hill was occupied for about 600 years. On a clear day the extensive views include Charnwood Forest and Leicester to the west, Melton Mowbray to the north, Billesdon Coplow to the south and Rutland to the east.

Since 1970 Burrough Hill has been leased and managed by Leicestershire County Council for the enjoyment of the public as an open space. This was made possible through the initiative of the Ernest Cook Trust which owns the hill and many of the adjoining farms as well as much of Little Dalby. The hill fort can be walked around during daylight hours and the are ramparts still impressive. A toposcope indicates many of the surrounding viewpoints.

The Leicestershire Round

Devised by the Leicestershire Footpath Association, The Leicestershire Round is a 100-mile walk around Leicestershire and Rutland. It follows an excellent network of footpaths and tracks, well-waymarked throughout. A publication entitled 'The Leicestershire Round' is available, detailing the whole route. This was updated in 1997 into one complete volume – three booklets were originally produced. The walk starts from the viewing point on Burrough Hill, and if you intend walking the whole of The Leicestershire Round as a long-distance walk, allow at least a week.

The Route

From Hollies Farm, turn right along the road to the road junction. Turn left along the quiet road towards Great Dalby, enjoying the view of the church nestling in the trees. Walk past Manor Farm, which supplies milk to Tuxford and Tebbutt, Melton Mowbray makers of Stilton and Leicester cheese. The farm was established in 1780 to produce milk for this company, which itself has existed for over 200 years.

Continue along the road, noting Burton Lazars Hall, then pass a pond where you may see a heron. Go uphill, enjoying the fine views of the undulating countryside and ignoring a track that leads up on to Gartree Hill. In a further 100 metres you reach a track, turn left, and walk ahead. After heavy rain this track is liable to be extremely muddy with puddles of water gathered in the farmer's tractor grooves. At a public footpath signpost, climb a small section of wooden fence and cross the grassy field to another public footpath signpost opposite. Turn left on to a green lane to follow a well-used path between two tall hedges. In places this grassy path will be muddy after a heavy downpour. At a group of farm buildings, join a surfaced track, ignoring a public footpath signpost near a small belt of trees. From here is a fine view of Burrough Hill and the escarpment.

At Moscow Farm, join a road towards Burrough which is embellished by a lawned verge each side. Walk along to its conclusion by Moscow Lodge. Turn left in the direction of Burrough once again, continuing along this road as far as a Leicestershire Round footpath signpost for Burrough Hill (½ mile). A grassy field track now leads ahead towards the escarpment, pinpointed by the toposcope. Pass through two wooden hand gates in quick succession to enter the country park. Tread carefully as there are many rabbit warrens tunnelled into the hillside. Cattle and sheep graze all over this area so if you have a dog with you please ensure that your pet is on a leash.

An obvious path winds uphill to the ramparts of the Iron Age hill fort. Go through the gap in the ramparts which is the entrance to the hill fort then follow the edge of the hill around to the right. Upon reaching Burrough Hill Covet, make your way downhill to a pair of wooden hand gates. Pass through the compound on to a well-walked path, now making for a stile by a large gate.

The entrance to the Dalby Hills path is via this stile. It is not a public right of way but members of the public are welcome to use it on foot or horseback, except at such times when it may be closed for the odd day each year. The path takes you through an extremely beautiful wood and is waymarked throughout. At the end of the wood, climb a stile. Continue ahead on a track, enjoying the views of Little Dalby ahead. At the end of Punch Bowl Covert is an obvious junction of tracks. Here turn left, leaving The Leicestershire Round and going downhill through a large, green gate.

Where the track goes to the left, climb a stile and follow a path enclosed by a fence and stream. Cross then join a field path that veers away diagonally to the road. The high wall of Little Dalby Hall is to

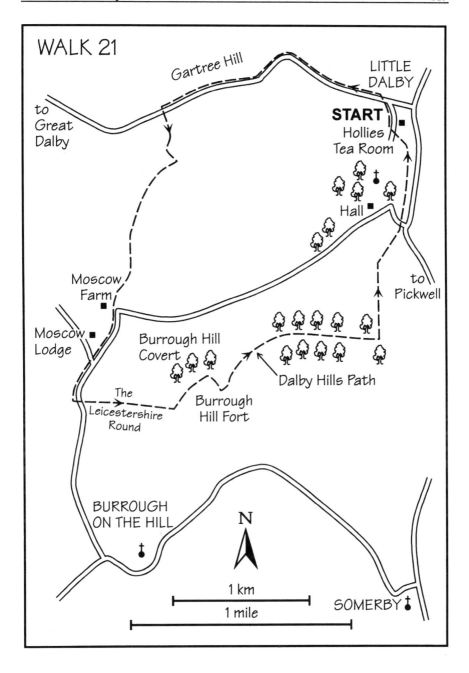

your left. On the opposite side of the road is a public footpath sign-post to Little Dalby. The parkland path is rather vague, but you need to head for a waymarker post then pass alongside a wood to a ditch which is guarded either side by a stile. Go uphill to the next way-marker post then cross the access road to the hall. From here the magnificent church stands proud, surrounded by trees.

Head downhill to a group of houses to locate a stile by a large, wooden gate. In 100 metres pass through a hand gate to the road. Turn right, passing Pepper's House, and in 50 metres you will come to Hollies Farm.

```
┌─────────────────────────────────────────────────────┐
│                                                       │
│           Walk 22. Cold Overton                       │
│                                                       │
└─────────────────────────────────────────────────────┘
```

Route: Gates Nurseries – Cold Overton – Radio Relay Station Mast – Windmill Lodge – Knossington – Gates' Nurseries Tea Shop.

Start: Gates Nurseries Garden Centre, Somerby Road, Cold Overton. GR 812099

Distance: 6 miles

Maps: OS Landrangers 130 Grantham and surrounding area and 141 Kettering, Corby and surrounding area. OS Explorer 15 Rutland Water and Stamford.

Terrain: Rolling hills and uplands. Mainly clear footpaths and bridleways. Paths from and to Cold Overton may be difficult to follow in summer because of high crops.

Public Transport: A very limited weekday service from Melton Mowbray to Cold Overton, operated by Blands and by Lincs Roadcar.

By Car: Cold Overton is two miles from Langham off the A606. There is plenty of free parking available at Gates Nurseries Garden Centre.

The Tea Shop

Gates Nurseries Tea Shop is located within the garden centre, at the far end of the very well organised nurseries. Looking at the tea shop you would think that it has been there a number of years, in fact, it was purpose-built in 1995, to blend in with the character of the garden centre. The tea shop has been built out of reclaimed materials, including a fine, old slate roof.

The tea shop inside features oak beams, a stone-flagged floor, pine furniture and an array of pictures and prints on the walls. The manageress, Yvonne Bryers, has her hands full as the tea shop seats up to 80 customers. At weekends it is quite possible for the tea shop to be full, but due to its layout you never get the feeling of being over-crowded. Everything is reasonably priced and the menu on offer includes morning coffee, light lunches, afternoon teas and home-made cakes. Two glass display cabinets are full of cakes and savouries and the staff provide a friendly service. Whether you are calling as a tourist or a local – a warm welcome awaits you.

Opening Hours: 10.00 – 17.30 Monday to Friday. 10.00 – 17.00 weekends and bank holiday Mondays. Telephone 01664 454309

Gates Nurseries Garden Centre

Set within a Victorian walled garden built in 1818, this was formerly the kitchen garden of Cold Overton Hall. The business was started in 1948 by Mr Frederick Arthur Gates, and continues to be a family concern. The nurseries have grown over the years to form a large, yet still friendly centre, offering advice on all gardening requirements. Indoors there is an extensive range of houseplants, tools and garden furniture. In the giftware department there is a large selection of silk flowers, candles, ceramics and glassware, cards and giftwrap. From the landscaped car park there are superb views of the nearby hills and countryside. The garden centre is open seven days a week, 08.00 – 18.00.

Welcome to Rutland!

Cold Overton

Cold Overton is four miles from Oakham and Rutland Water, situated just inside Leicestershire, and about three-quarters of a mile from the border with Rutland. From the village's lofty perch there are magnificent views of Melton District to the west and Rutland to the east. St John the Baptist's Church, with its tall spire, is mainly 13th century. The church is famous for the number of stone and wooden carvings of heads and figures, both internally and externally.

Knossington

A small, charming village, some 600 feet (183m) above sea level and clustered around St Peter's Church. The village in early times belonged to Owston Abbey, and upon the Dissolution passed into the hands of Gregory, Lord Cromwell, son of Thomas Cromwell. Do visit the 12th-century church. It has many jewels – especially the Early English font, which is one of the finest in the county. Knossington is a favourite with the Cottesmore Hunt so keep an eye out for this spectacular sight as you make your way through the countryside around the village.

The Route

Go out of the entrance to the garden centre to cross Somerby Road to Main Street. In 150 metres turn right at a public footpath signpost, on to a gravelled track. Go through the wooden gate and walk ahead as directed by the yellow waymarker arrow over two small, grassy fields. Locate a public footpath signpost in the hedge.

Cross the road to another public footpath signpost about 50 metres to the left. The path runs diagonally over this field to a large double gate in the right-hand corner. This field may be difficult to cross if the farmer has planted a high crop such as rape seed. Continue ahead as before, making for a field hedge corner in the direction of the radio relay station mast. In a further 50 metres, ahead of you is a single wooden stile in a wire mesh fence. Aim for a large, metal gate in the right-hand hedge of the next field. However, once you have crossed the brook, ignore the gate, and continue over the field by the hedge and road to the far corner of the field.

Pass through the wooden swing gate by the public footpath signpost and out on to the road. You have now entered Rutland. Turn left along the road, climbing uphill, as far as the radio relay station mast. Turn right at the public bridleway signpost on to a track. You reach a wooden gate by the enclosed reservoir. From this point there is a panoramic view of Rutland Water from a very unusual angle.

The track leads around to the right to a wooden swing gate where a blue waymarker arrow points the way ahead. Follow alongside the field perimeter hedge, eventually making for a large gap in the hedge and ignoring a path off to the right. Continue on in the same manner, by the hedge, to come to a wooden swing gate. Pass through this gate then immediately through the next swing gate, 50 metres to the left. An enclosed path now leads ahead between two tall hedges.

This area seems to be very popular with long-tailed tits, which can be seen going about their business in the hedgerows. It is also a popular bridleway with horses so do not be surprised to find it very muddy in wet weather. Pass through a wooden swing gate, noting Flitteriss Park Farm nestling away in the beautiful countryside. The bridleway opens out quite dramatically before the next swing gate. Make then for the right-hand of two gates ahead before following alongside the hedge, through an open gateway to a slightly larger gate by the road.

Cross Braunston Road to rejoin the bridleway, which is very easy to follow ahead. At the stream, cross either by the ford or walking the plank, then go uphill slightly to your left to a farm gate. Walk alongside a mature hedge for the length of the field to a swing gate. A rough, grassy field path takes you round the field perimeter hedge to the next gate. Head diagonally over a small field as instructed by the waymarker arrow, noting the village of Knossington. You are now back in Leicestershire, although there is no official boundary point to advise you in these fields.

At an obvious junction of bridleways, turn right on to a clear path alongside a hedge. Continue into the next field along a farm track, going downhill to a stream. At this point you are again at the county border with Rutland. A field path now leads uphill to Windmill Lodge then passes to the left of the beautiful ironstone farmhouse which was built in 1851. This was the old miller's cottage that stood next to the windmill – unfortunately no longer there. A wide, grassy track now leads away from the farmhouse to a metal farm gate. Cross

WALK 22

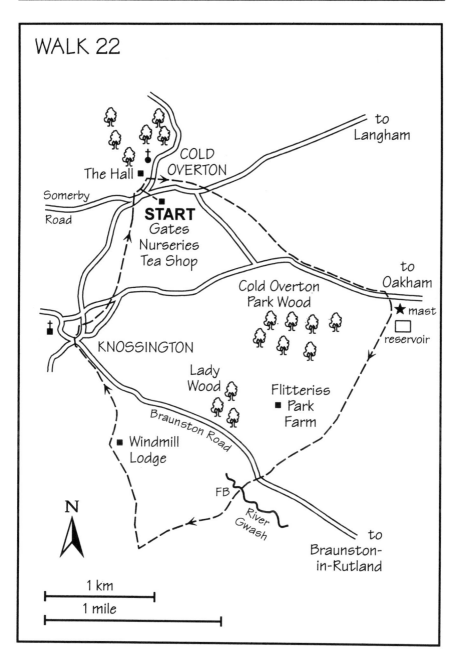

to
Langham

COLD
OVERTON

The Hall ■

Somerby
Road

■ **START**
Gates
Nurseries
Tea Shop

Cold Overton
Park Wood

to
Oakham

★ mast

□
reservoir

KNOSSINGTON

Lady
Wood

Flitteriss
■ Park
Farm

Braunston Road

■ Windmill
Lodge

FB

River
Gwash

to
Braunston-
in-Rutland

N

1 km

1 mile

a stream then pass through a succession of gates to reach the village of Knossington.

Turn left along Braunston Road and go as far as the road junction. Go right towards Oakham along Main Street, following round into Cold Overton Road. A public footpath signpost and stile will be located opposite Larchwood Rise. Cross the field in the direction of the signpost to a wooden stile set in a wire mesh fence. You may well have to fight your way through an overgrown copse for the 50 metres to the road.

Pass through a wooden gate into the field opposite to climb a wooden fence in front of you. Cross the next field to the hedge opposite then make for the next wooden fence ahead. Climb, cross the next field to a large hedge gap, where there will probably be no obvious path over the field. Aim for the houses of Cold Overton opposite, then as you get nearer head for the Dutch barn at Manor Farm. Turn right along the road for 100 metres, to a road junction. Turn right along Somerby Road to return to Gates Nurseries.

```
┌──────────────────────────────────────────────────────────────┐
│                                                                │
│              Walk 23. Wymondham                                │
│                                                                │
└──────────────────────────────────────────────────────────────┘
```

Route: Wymondham Windmill – Wymondham – Blue Point Farm – Woodwell Head – Edmonthorpe – Wymondham – Windmill Tea Room.

Start: Wymondham Windmill, Butt Lane, Wymondham. GR 850193

Distance: 7¾ miles

Maps: OS Landranger 130 Grantham and surrounding area and OS Pathfinder 876 Wymondham and Cottesmore.

Terrain: Level walking over field footpaths, bridleways and tracks. Pleasant woodland path through Woodwell Head Plantation.

Public Transport: A regular Melton Mowbray to Corby 'Rutland Flyer' service, operated jointly by Midland Fox and Blands. No Sunday service.

By Car: Wymondham is situated two and a half miles off the B676 Melton Mowbray to Colsterworth road. Travelling from Melton Mowbray, after passing signs for Stapleford Park, look out for the turning to Wymondham just before Saxby. Parking is available at the windmill.

The Tea Shop

The Windmill Tea Room at Wymondham Windmill has been established since 1990. The current proprietor, Vincent Manchester, took over in 1993. All the old mill buildings were taken down then rebuilt into craft workshops and the tea room. They are now totally unrecognisable. Inside the tea room you will not be disappointed. The oak-beamed ceiling helps create the traditional tea shop image. Prints and original paintings decorate the walls, while baking accessories hang from the ceiling as decorations.

Vincent bakes all the cakes himself, rising at a very early hour each day. Home-made soups, toasted sandwiches, beans on toast and a selection of sandwiches are available, together with a delicious array of scrumptious cakes for the day. Cream teas with lashings of jam and cream are his forte. There is seating for a maximum of 50, with bookings essential for groups. On sunny days tables are placed by the windmill, but do look out as you may have to share your tea with the chickens and ducks that roam around the mill!

Opening Hours: 10.00 – 17.30 Tuesday to Sunday and bank holiday Mondays. Open at weekends only from November to February inclusive. Telephone: 01572 787304.

Wymondham Windmill

Standing on a hill overlooking Wymondham is a handsome, five-storey, ironstone windmill. Built in 1814, the windmill is in the process of being restored by its owner, David Towndrow, and is one of only four six-sailed mills remaining in the country. It is known as a Six Arm Lincolnshire Cross. After its complete restoration, it will grind flour again. In the meantime you can visit the windmill and climb to the top. All David asks is a donation to its restoration. The craft workshops for traditional mill crafts are by the windmill and are also worth exploring. There is also a children's play area to keep the younger members of the family happy.

Wymondham

Wymondham is six miles from Melton Mowbray. For centuries a weekly market was held in the wide Main Street. An annual fair was granted in 1303, but today the village is considerably smaller. Roman remains have been found here in the form of a pavement and other relics. The large parish church of St Peter has a 13th-century chancel with a number of monuments to the Berkeley family, Lords of the Manor until 1630. An interesting building next to the church is the Free School, which was built in 1637 as a Grammar School. In 1885 it was renovated to be used as a reading room for the village.

However, Wymondham, like Little Dalby, is famous for manufacturing Stilton cheese. Many believe Mrs Paulet of Wymondham was the first to make Stilton cheese. She supplied it to her brother-in-law, landlord at the Bell Inn at Stilton on the Great North Road. He sold the cheese to travellers in 1730 with the village name being adopted for the cheese. Even before this date this beautiful cheese was known as Quenby cheese or Lady Beaumont's cheese, but that's quite a different story!

Edmonthorpe

With a population of less than 100, this village was originally a Danish settlement. Houses and cottages are scattered around the green

Edmonthorpe village pump dates from 1858

lanes that lead to the 'drift', a medieval drove road. The church of St Michael is rather grand, especially for the size of the village. The ironstone tower dates to the 13th century while the rest of the church is 15th-century. Nearby are the ruins of Edmonthorpe Hall. Before being destroyed by fire in 1943, the hall's last inhabitants were prisoners from the Second World War.

The Route

From the windmill, turn right on to Butt Lane and follow the road downhill to the junction by the Berkeley Arms in Wymondham village. Turn left, heading out of Wymondham and passing Park Cottages (1881), to a public footpath signpost for Buckminster.

Walk over a field as shown, passing just to the right of a small pond. Climb a stile then go through a wooden swing gate and up on to the old railway trackbed. Turn right, then in 10 metres turn left through a hedge to reach a junction of paths. Follow along the field perimeter hedge on the obvious path, which is well waymarked with yellow-topped posts. At the next junction of footpaths, climb a stile into the next field, ignoring the path that departs towards the road.

Climb a stile then cross a wooden, one-hand footbridge, walking alongside a stream to come to yet another junction of paths. Cross the footbridge and turn immediately right over two concrete slabs over the stream you were following. A path leads up the right-hand side of the field as far as the road. Turn left and walk along the road for 300 metres to locate a public bridleway signpost. Amazingly, after the distance that you have travelled, the windmill can still be seen, behind, on the sky line.

A track is followed for 150 metres then you need to turn left at the blue waymarker arrow on a post, which may be hidden in the hedgerow. Cross the field on the obvious path, which is liberally dented by horses' hooves. Pass through a large hedge gap then follow the field around to the right, passing by Marriott's Spinney. Go over the next field as shown to another large gap. Continue around to the right of the next field, ensuring that you follow alongside a hedge.

Cross a farmer's track then turn right as shown by the arrow on the waymarker post, now walking adjacent to the farmer's track. Pass through a large hedge gap where a field path leads to a group of trees ahead. Continue forward along a grassy path which is bounded by a hedge each side. A field perimeter path then brings you to a junction of paths and track. Turn right, straight off the track on to a grassy field path. Walk alongside a mature hedge. Pass by the entrance to Blue Point Farm to join a byway that leads to the road.

Turn right and walk along the road for 350 metres to find a public footpath signpost at the entrance to Pasture Farm. Walk along the access drive as far as the dismantled railway bridge. Climb the stile to continue along by the hedge to reach two stiles by the farm house. Cross the field heading for the far right-hand corner. Join a farm track. Turn right, then in 200 metres negotiate an old, wooden gate, turning left on to another track. Walk ahead then follow it round to the right. Where the track turns to the left, leave it to join a field perimeter path. In a quarter of a mile, follow alongside Woodwell Head Wood to a junction of bridleways.

Turn right into the wood. A wooden bridge gives you access to a beautiful woodland path. At the end of the wood a green track leads ahead towards Hall Farm. The track cuts away to the left of the farm then bears to the right, passing beneath the farmhouse. When reaching the track that goes to the farm, turn left and follow this track for

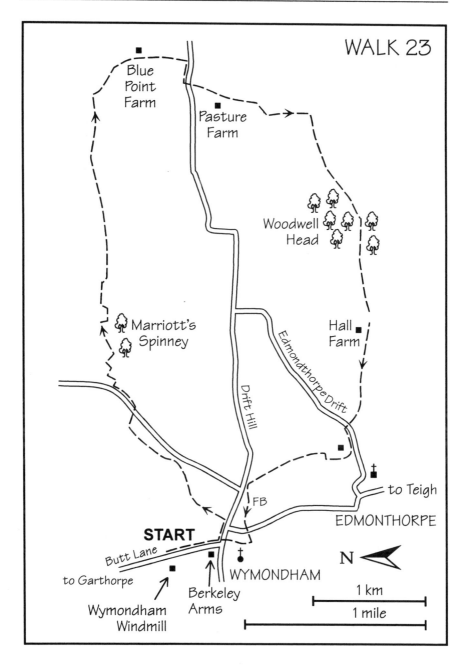

WALK 23

Blue Point Farm

Pasture Farm

Woodwell Head

Marriott's Spinney

Hall Farm

Edmondthorpe Drift

Drift Hill

to Teigh

EDMONTHORPE

FB

START

Butt Lane

to Garthorpe

Wymondham Windmill

Berkeley Arms

WYMONDHAM

N

1 km

1 mile

half a mile into Woodwell Head Lane and the village of Edmonthorpe.

Turn left by Edmonthorpe Social Club, heading into the village as far as Manor Farm. Turn right at the public bridleway signpost on to a thin path which may be overgrown in summer. At a junction of paths, continue ahead on the path bounded by a tall hedge. Follow the path around to the right then left, passing beneath a beautiful archway of trees. After a quarter of a mile, go through a wooden hand gate to cross a grassy field to the next hand gate. A wide track then takes you towards the road.

Take an obvious thin path off the track, making for Wymondham church. Cross the stream either by the ford or concrete footbridge, walking ahead for a further 300 metres into Wymondham village. Cross Edmonthorpe Road into Nurses Lane, passing the entrance to the church. At Main Street, turn left and walk back to the Berkeley Arms. Retrace your footsteps up Butt Lane to the windmill and a delicious treat at the tea room.

Walk 24. Uppingham

Route: Baines Tea Room – Uppingham – Lyddington – Stoke Dry Wood – Uppingham School – Baines Tea Room.

Start: Baines Tea Room, High Street West, Uppingham. GR 866998

Distance: 5½ miles

Maps: OS Landranger 141 Kettering, Corby and surrounding area, OS Pathfinder 917 Corby (North) and Uppingham and OS Explorer 15 Rutland Water and Stamford.

Terrain: Well-used paths and tracks, which may be muddy in places after heavy rain. Steep climb to the top of the Uppingham uplands at Lyddington.

Public Transport: A fairly frequent Rutland Flyer service between Corby and Melton Mowbray via Uppingham, operated by Midland Fox.

By Car: Uppingham straddles the A6003 Oakham to Corby road. It can also be reached using the A47 Leicester to Peterborough road. There are two free car parks in Uppingham, both on North Street East.

The Tea Shop

Baines Tea Room is part of Baines Bakery and is on the corner of High Street West and London Road in the centre of Uppingham. The building dates back to the 17th century and the tea room has been operating since 1965. The Bakery and Tea Room is owned by Mrs Baines, with all cakes, scones and rolls being baked in the bakery and served in the tea room.

Breakfast is served from 9.00 to 11.00, while lunch is available between 12 noon and 14.00. Rolls and sandwiches are on the menu all day. A super selection of Twinning Speciality Teas is available and there is even a choice of herbal teas. Tempting home-made cakes and scones can be enjoyed from the sweet trolley. For aficionados of cream teas, these are highly recommended, although slightly expensive.

The tea room surroundings are most congenial. A wooden-beamed, low ceiling, decorative walls and quaint tables add to the charm and atmosphere that has been created over the years – very

much in character with the town itself. It is a tribute to the tea room
that you could be lulled into thinking that you are in the Peak District or Yorkshire Dales rather than Rutland.

Opening Hours: 9.00 – 17.00 Monday to Saturday. Closed Sundays and bank holidays. Telephone 01572 823317

Uppingham

This small market town is six miles from Oakham along the A6003.
It is Rutland's second town and full of character and unspoilt charm.
Uppingham stands on a steep hill and is dominated by the attractive
building of the public school. The long High Street, with its narrow
back alleys, contains many interesting small shops and pubs which
just have to be explored. Uppingham is absolutely typical of the traditional image of a small English market town that is now becoming
increasingly difficult to find.

The centrepiece of the town is the Market Place, where a stall
market takes place every Friday. Behind The Vaults pub, the spire of
the parish church rises up and the porch of the church is situated

The beautiful cricket pavillion at Uppingham

just to the side of the old inn. The church dates to the 14th century, having been restored and enlarged in 1860. Inside the church are early 13th-century half-figures of Christ, a saint and two angels.

Uppingham school's buildings date from 1594. It was founded by Archdeacon Robert Johnson as the town's grammar school. During the 19th century the school developed to become an important public school and now there are over 600 pupils, 126 of whom are girls. Guided tours show visitors inside seven of the central buildings which are of historical and architectural interest. Tours take place on Saturdays from mid-June until mid-September and further details are available by telephoning 01572 822676 or 822216.

Lyddington

The village of Lyddington is one of the finest villages in Rutland. Along Main Street are many attractive ironstone houses and cottages, some with date stones of the 17th and 18th centuries. There is a pretty village green and a 13th-century market cross.

While in Lyddington, Bede House must be visited. Rebuilt in the 15th century, it was for many centuries before a palace of the Bishops of Lincoln, certainly from the reign of King John (1199-1216). In 1602 the son of William Cecil of Burghley, the second Lord Burghley, converted it into an almshouse. The name of Bede House dates from this time as the residents were expected to pray ('biddan') for their benefactors. English Heritage administers the house, which is open to the public between April and September. For details telephone 01572 822438.

The Route

From Baines Tea Room at the junction of High Street West and London Road, make for the church, walking along London Road as far as South View. Turn left in 50 metres at a public footpath signpost for Lyddington. Join the footpath as it descends to a stile and a stream. Continue uphill to the next stile, where a field perimeter path is now followed. Pass through a small wood then turn left on to a green track by The Knoll.

In 100 metres turn right at the public footpath signpost and descend a field alongside a hedge. Cross a stream to go uphill to the school playing fields. On the extreme left is a stile set in a wooden

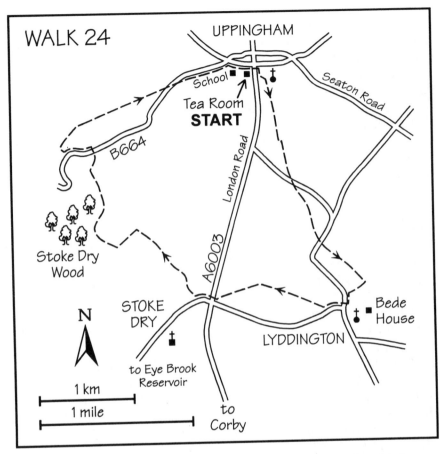

WALK 24

UPPINGHAM

School

Seaton Road

Tea Room
START

B664

London Road

A6003

Stoke Dry
Wood

N

STOKE
DRY

LYDDINGTON

Bede
House

to Eye Brook
Reservoir

1 km

1 mile

to
Corby

fence next to a telegraph pole. Cross another green track, which may
be overgrown, to a stile then bear half-left to the next stile and road.
A public footpath signpost will be found opposite where you need to
join a field path to the immediate left, heading towards Lyddington,
which is ahead in the valley.

Continue downhill in the direction of the church to reach a fence.
A little further ahead and you will be standing on the road again.
Cross to rejoin the field path that takes you over a number of stiles
and alongside two ponds. Cross a stream and several more stiles to
come to a track and a wooden public footpath signpost. Turn right
along the track then a lane to pass the children's playing area to
reach the centre of Lyddington village.

Turn left along the main road through the village and go as far as the road junction turning to the right to Stoke Dry. Go along Stoke Road and at the last house in the village turn right at a public footpath signpost. Walk ahead, then climb the steep hill on the obvious path to the top. At a wooden swing gate, do look back at the view of the uplands of Rutland and Lyddington village below. On a clear day Seaton Viaduct will be spied in the Welland Valley.

Cross the busy A6003 to a minor road that leads to Stoke Dry. This village is famous for the home of the Gunpowder Plot to destroy Parliament. Pass through a gate on to a bridleway and walk along a wide, grassy path with a hedge to your left. Continue over an open field, bearing left to a wooden gate where a defined path goes between a hedge and wire fence. From here there is magnificent view of Eye Brook reservoir which was used as a training ground for the Dam Busters Raid in 1943.

Upon reaching Stoke Dry Wood, follow round to the right ensuring that you do not turn left into the wood. A very obvious grassy path takes you by the north-east tip of the wood on to a gravelled track. Follow this track for a quarter of a mile to the B664 Stockerstone road. Turn left along the road to a point where it turns sharply to the left. Here, turn right along a farm track, then bear right on to field path before reaching the farmyard.

As you walk along the field footpath over the grassy fields there are good views of Wardley Wood and Wardley village. Climb a stile on your right then continue ahead, as indicated by the waymarker arrows, over a number of fields to rejoin the B664. Turn left along the road into Uppingham for a very pleasant walk through the small town. The road leads into High Street West and passes Uppingham School before Baines Bakery and Tea Room are returned to in the town centre.

```
┌─────────────────────────────────────────────────────────────┐
│                                                               │
│                    Walk 25. Oakham                            │
│                                                               │
└─────────────────────────────────────────────────────────────┘
```

Route: The Barn at Furleys – Oakham – Brooke – Gunthorpe Hall – Rutland Water Nature Reserve – Egleton – Oakham – The Barn at Furleys.

Start: Burley Road car park, Oakham. GR 864088.

Distance: 6¾ miles

Maps: OS Landranger 141 Kettering, Corby and surrounding area, OS Pathfinder 896 Rutland Water and OS Explorer 15 Rutland Water and Stamford.

Terrain: Good, clear paths and tracks throughout. Walk through Nature Reserve – no dogs allowed. Interesting stroll around part of Oakham.

Public Transport: Oakham railway station is served by regular train services from Leicester and Peterborough. Good bus service to Oakham from Melton Mowbray, Corby and Stamford, operated by different bus companies.

By Car: Oakham may be reached by the A47 Leicester to Peterborough road via the A6003 from Uppingham. The A606 Melton Mowbray to Stamford road passes through the town centre. There are a number of free car parks dotted about the town, all well-signposted.

The Tea Shop

The Barn at Furleys is a special tea shop in a special town. This is a luxurious tea shop of the highest quality but, as you might expect, it is not cheap. Previously an old barn, Furleys opened in 1992, just around the corner from the other two family-run businesses.

The licensed tea shop is on a split level with tables placed elegantly within the serving area. Hand-knitted flowers grace the tables, which are beautifully covered with expensive tablecloths and napkins. All around you are gift ideas of painted pottery and the decor of the tea shop is first class. There is a remarkable range of food on offer with lunches served from 12 noon to 14.30. If you intend eating at lunch time you will need to book ahead. Home-made cakes, cream teas, a choice of teas and coffees are all available, and a visit is a 'must' while in Oakham.

Opening Hours: 12.00 – 16.45 (last orders) Monday. 09.30 – 16.45 (last orders) Tuesday to Saturday. Closed on Sundays. Telephone 01572 770245

Oakham

Once again Oakham is the county town of Rutland after 23 years as part of Leicestershire. The town nestles in the beautiful Vale of Catmose, at the head of Rutland Water. It is a place where you instantly feel at home, with many old-fashioned shops that are a delight to look over. A street market is held in the Market Place twice weekly, on Wednesdays and Saturdays. Here also is the historic buttercross. This is the last surviving market cross in the town. At one time there were four, standing at the four corners of Oakham. Anyone with an interest in model railways must view Oakham signal box. The signal box was used by Hornby as an original for their model.

Oakham Castle was built in 1191. Only the Great Hall remains. Housed inside is a unique collection of horseshoes decorated with coats of arms. The collection goes back many hundreds of years, and

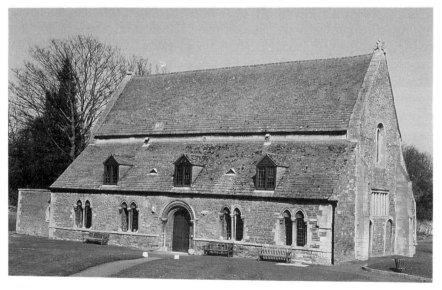

Of Oakham Castle, only the Great Hall remains

it is an ancient custom that every peer passing through Oakham should forfeit a horseshoe to the Lord of the Manor. In recent years the main contributors have been the royal family when they have visited Oakham. If you wish to see the 200 plus horseshoes, the castle is open every day except Monday. Telephone 01572 723654.

The Rutland County Museum on Catmos Street portrays the life of Rutland through the centuries. The building itself is most remarkable. Built in the 18th century as an indoor riding school for a local troop of part-time soldiers known as The Rutland Fencibles, it was constructed under a huge, self-supporting, timber roof to enable the horses to have room to manoeuvre when being trained in the arts of cavalry horsemanship. On display are local crafts and craft tools, archaeological finds from Rutland Water site, agricultural implements, equipment and wagons. Open daily except Mondays and winter Sundays. Telephone 01572 723654.

Brooke

Brooke is no more than a hamlet, but it is one of Rutland's loveliest. The church of St Peter has a Norman doorway and a tower built in the 13th century. The north aisle and chapel and the chancel were all rebuilt in 1579 by the Noel family. The church, the Old Rectory, which is the oldest house in the village, and a handful of houses are all that remain of this shrunken village which was much larger in the 12th century when an Augustinian priory existed.

Gunthorpe

Around Gunthorpe Hall are traces of the lost village of Gunthorpe. As you approach the hall there are signs of ridge and furrow, while considerable earthworks can be seen to the left of the hall, all indicating the site of the former village. Gunthorpe was mentioned in a forest perambulation in 1218, but by 1665 had only one resident other than the occupants of the hall.

Rutland Water Nature Reserve

Entrance to the reserve may be made at Egleton or Lyndon. The reserve covers an area of 182 hectares (450 acres) along the nine miles of shoreline of the reservoir. There are 17 hides that look out over three lagoons and open water. Created at the same time the reservoir was constructed, it is managed by the Leicestershire and Rutland Trust for Nature Conservation on behalf of Anglian Water. The following birds are present all year round: gadwall, shoveler, teal, tufted duck, pochard and shelduck. In winter they are joined by pintail, goldeneye, goosander, wigeon and many other rarer visitors. To safeguard wildlife and grazing sheep, dogs are not allowed at Egleton reserve, while at Lyndon reserve they must be on a lead. Day permits are necessary and are available from the visitors' centre. Telephone 01572 770651.

The Route

From the entrance to Burley Road car park, turn right along Burley Road, passing the tea room to reach the roundabout at High Street in the centre of Oakham. Cross to Mill Street opposite, then continue ahead into Brooke Road. Once over the railway crossing, turn left to Brooke and head out of Oakham into the beautiful, open countryside. The road goes uphill sharply but the climb is worthwhile as there is a fine view of Oakham behind.

Turn left at a public bridleway footpath signpost on to a track which may be muddy in places, especially after heavy rain. From here you can see Burley on the Hill House and Rutland Water Reservoir. Where the track bears to the left to join a grassy path, turn right through a wooden gate. Keep to the left as you descend a grassy field, now making for Brooke, below in the distance. Pass through two grey gates in fairly quick succession, noting that you are now walking along the MacMillan Way.

The path squeezes between two hedges before a wide track is joined at Hillside Cottage. At the bottom of the hill, just before the lane that leads into Brooke, turn left at a public bridleway footpath signpost to Gunthorpe (1 mile). Briefly follow alongside a stream then a grassy track brings you to an old, metal farm gate. Pass through and turn left on to an obvious field perimeter path next to a hedge. This path then leads on to a farmer's concrete track, which in turn brings you to a cattle grid. Turn right as indicated to a sturdy, green gate and entrance to Gunthorpe Estate.

Pass by the old stables of the hall and Groome's Cottage to a triangle of estate roads. Gunthorpe Hall will be seen here but you must bear to the left along the driveway. In 200 metres turn right through a large, green, double gate on to an obvious field perimeter path. Skirt alongside a wood then turn into the wood on a wide path. Turn right through a large gap before going downhill to the gated railway level crossing. Take care over the railway lines. In 100 metres the A6003 is reached.

Turn right along the road for 200 metres to the entrance to Rutland Water Nature Reserve. Join the reservoir perimeter track that takes you into the wildfowl sanctuary where dogs are not allowed. You are now sharing the track with cyclists that are following the 17 or 23-mile perimeter cycleway that encompasses the whole of Rutland Water. The larger route takes cyclists around the Hambleton Peninsula.

No directions need to be given as the circuit track is very evident from here to the car park for Egleton Birdwatching Centre. However, do enjoy the views of Rutland Water and keep a sharp eye out for wildlife. Turn left at the car park and go along the cycle track which runs alongside Hambleton Road into Egleton village.

Turn right along Church Road and walk through the pretty village of Egleton as far as St Edmund's Church. By the church is the tiny, former village school, erected by the Finch family in 1867. Turn left at a public footpath signpost opposite the church on to a farmer's track. Follow alongside a hedge, then cross an open field to join a hedge again, where a metal kissing gate will be located. Pass through on to a well-walked path that crosses a pleasant, green field to a stile and a public footpath signpost.

Here, turn right along the A6003, crossing Swooning Bridge. Do look at the parapets engraved with initials of lovers – it was here that swains would bring their girls in olden times. Continue on, passing the Rutland County Museum, to Burley Road where The Barn at Furleys will be found. The car park is 100 metres past the entrance to the tea shop.

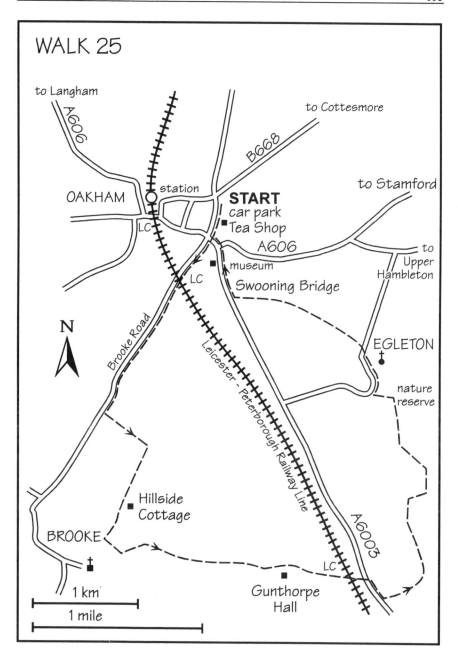

WALK 25

to Langham

A606

to Cottesmore

B668

to Stamford

OAKHAM

station

LC

START
car park
Tea Shop

A606

to
Upper
Hambleton

museum

LC

Swooning Bridge

N

Brooke Road

Leicester - Peterborough Railway Line

EGLETON

nature
reserve

Hillside
Cottage

BROOKE

A6003

LC

Gunthorpe
Hall

1 km
1 mile

Walk 26. Ashwell

Route: Rutland Garden Centre – Ashwell Road – Langham – Burley Road – Oakham Disused Canal – Ruby's Tea Room – Rutland Garden Centre.

Start: Rutland Garden Centre, Ashwell Road, Oakham. The garden centre is midway between Ashwell and Oakham. GR 867120

Distance: 5¼ miles

Maps: OS Landranger 130 Grantham and surrounding area and OS Explorer 15 Rutland Water and Stamford.

Terrain: Mainly flat walking along well-used field bridleways and footpaths. A little road walking with a short section by a disused canal.

Public Transport: A frequent service (number 2) between Nottingham Broad Marsh and Oakham passes the garden centre. The service is operated by Barton Buses.

By Car: The garden centre can be reached by taking the A606 Melton to Oakham road as far as Langham then following signs for Burley, turning left by Ashwell Prison towards Ashwell. From Oakham, just follow the signposted road to Ashwell for two miles. Parking is available at the garden centre car park.

The Tea Shop

Ruby's Tea Room is part of Rutland Garden Centre and has been open since 1993. Ruby Hamilton owns and runs the tea room, and in her words it is 'small and cosy'. It is a delightful tea room with a beamed ceiling, prints on the wall and immaculate curtains at the windows. There is only room for 25 patrons at the six tables, but the extension to the garden centre has been a worthwhile addition.

All cakes are home-made with a good choice available every day. Ruby's cream teas are exceptional and thoroughly recommended. If you are feeling hungry after the walk, why not try one of her snacks. There are sandwiches, pies, Cornish pasties and jacket potatoes with interesting fillings to choose from. Whatever you pick from the menu you are assured of a good feast. Good food and a warm welcome make this a tea room not to be missed.

Opening Hours: 10.00 – 17.00, every day except Tuesday. Closed first two weeks in July, one week at Christmas and New Year. Telephone 01572 723583

Ruby's Tea Room at Rutland Garden Centre, Ashwell

Rutland Garden Centre

This is an impressive little garden centre, owned by Brian Hamilton, which has everything for the gardener. Opened in 1976, the garden centre was built on land belonging to two cottages. Next door is a conservatory centre owned by Brian's son. The garden centre is open Monday to Friday 08.00 – 18.00, weekends 09.00 – 18.00. Closed for one week at Christmas.

Langham

Langham is a growing village, two miles north of Oakham. The church of St Peter and St Paul was originally a chapelry of Oakham, with much in common with its mother church. It is well worth looking over, as are the old, stone cottages in the older part of the village.

This village is home to Rutland's only brewery – Ruddles Brewery Ltd. There has been a brewery on the present site since 1858. Originally owned by the Parry family, it was obviously called Parry's. In 1922 Sir Kenneth Ruddle joined the board of directors and the name later changed to G Ruddle & Son. Eventually his son took control, but in 1992 the company was sold to Grolsch, a Danish firm, thus ending this family-run concern. The brewery has 100 employees and still brews County and Best Bitter ales. Parties of 15 can visit the brewery by appointment at £10.00 per head, which includes the tour, supper and as much beer as you can drink. Telephone 01572 756911 for further details. Individuals are not allowed but you may be able to join a party already booked on a tour.

Ashwell

Situated in the Vale of Catmos, Ashwell has an old wishing well from which the village takes its name. Reputedly, this old, holy well stands at the head of a magical spring and has a moral inscription above the well head. Opposite H M Ashwell Open Prison are the famous Cottesmore Hunt kennels.

The Oakham Canal

The Melton Mowbray to Oakham Canal was built at the end of the 18th century, at the peak of canal construction. With the advent of railways the canal was bought by the owners of the new Midland Railway Company. In 1846 the canal closed after a very short life as the railway company did not like competition. Today only a small part of the disused canal can be walked in the Oakham area.

The Route

From Rutland Garden Centre, turn right on to Ashwell Road, passing four cottages at Langham Place. These terraced cottages were built at the turn of the 20th century with the last cottage originally constructed as a pub called The Tambourine. In 200 metres turn left on to a track crossing Tambourine Bridge, which spans the Melton to Peterborough railway line.

The track narrows into a thin, grassy path that is bordered by a hedge and fence. At a junction of paths do not climb the stile but turn right to continue along the well-used bridleway. Continue ahead in the direction as before, taking care if walking after heavy rain as the path will be very muddy. Go by a small wood where the path rises slightly to bring you to Ashwell Road. Turn right, then in

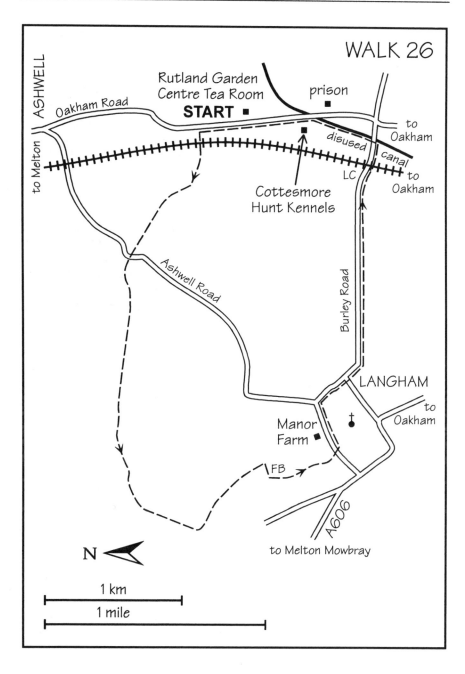

WALK 26

ASHWELL

to Melton

Oakham Road

Rutland Garden
Centre Tea Room
START ■

prison ■

to Oakham

disused canal

LC

to Oakham

Cottesmore
Hunt Kennels

Ashwell Road

Burley Road

LANGHAM

to Oakham

Manor
Farm ■

†

FB

A606

to Melton Mowbray

N

1 km

1 mile

50 metres turn left by a pair of large field gates to rejoin the bridle-way.

Walk ahead as before, passing through a pretty wood. From the path there is powerful view of Langham village dominated by the church, nestling in the valley. Negotiate an old farm gate where a thin field perimeter path leads ahead. Follow along the edge of several fields, enjoying the satisfying views of the Rutland countryside. Enter a long, thin wood which in summer may be overgrown in places. Ignore a small farm gate on the left as you make your way through this small, enclosed wood, eventually emerging on a field perimeter path.

A very long walk over a field brings you to a junction with a green track. Bear left, keeping close to the hedge, and continuing ahead for a quarter of a mile to reach an old pair of wooden stiles in the hedge. Climb, then follow the path by a ditch, heading towards your guiding star of Langham church in the distance. Cross two wooden planks over a ditch then at the end of the field turn right by an old wooden public footpath signpost. In 200 metres turn left across a fine, wooden footbridge, well-hidden in the hedge. Go diagonally over the next field to a yellow-topped waymarker post. Follow alongside the hedge then round to the right of a field which may well be cordoned off due to horses in the field. In the right-hand corner of the field a stile leads you out on to a road in Langham village.

Turn left along the road into the village, passing Manor Farm and stables on your way to the road junction. Turn right on to Ashwell Road and follow as far as the crossroads in the village. Take the left-hand fork, signposted to Burley, and walk along the road out of Langham. In a further half mile you will come to Langham Junction level crossing. Take care in crossing the railway line then continue on for a additional 350 metres to locate a public footpath signpost by the disused Oakham canal.

Descend seven steps then climb a stile which gives access to the footpath alongside the old waterway. Cross a springy, wooden footbridge then tread with care along the path. All too quickly a large stile will be reached at the end of the disused canal, next to the road opposite HM Ashwell Prison. Turn left and walk along the road, passing Cottesmore Kennels and continuing for another quarter mile to return to Rutland Garden Centre.

Walk 27. Greetham

Route: Greetham Garden Centre – Greetham – Greetham Valley Golf Course – Fort Henry Lake – Exton Park – Viking Way – Greetham – Greetham Garden Centre Tea Room.

Start: Greetham Garden Centre, Oakham Road, Greetham. GR 923144

Distance: 6 miles

Maps: OS Landranger 130 Grantham and surrounding area and OS Explorer 15 Rutland Water and Stamford.

Terrain: Good, clear paths and tracks. Flat walking through beautiful countryside. No climbs.

Public Transport: A fairly regular Cottesmore – Greetham – Stamford service is operated by Blands of Oakham.

By Car: Greetham is close to the A1. From Stamford leave at Stretton to join the B668 into Greetham, or from Oakham follow the B668 through Burley and Cottesmore, which will bring you to the garden centre in Greetham.

The Tea Shop

Greetham Garden Centre Tea Room is owned and run by David Penny with a little help from his staff. The brick tea room was built on to the end of the garden centre and opened in 1994. Value for money, home-made fare is the principal on which the tea shop is run. A local lady who really enjoys cooking and likes experimenting makes the cakes for the tea room every second day. Hence the different and unusual cakes on show in the warm and friendly tea room.

There are only four tables inside the tea room, while outside in the conservatory and garden centre are many more. In fact, David is in the throes of extending the tea garden quite dramatically. The menu is restricted to tea or coffee, home-made cakes, sandwiches, snacks and jacket potatoes with a range of fillings. It is unbelievable that in this day and age you can purchase tea for two and a cake each for as little as £2.00! David really does ensure that that prices are kept very reasonable and rarely introduces a price increase. Well done!

Opening Hours: 9.00 – 17.00 weekdays and Saturdays. 10.00 – 18.00 Sundays. Telephone 01572 813100

Chris Lawton runs the Rutland Falconry and Owl Centre at Greenham
Garden Centre

Greetham Garden Centre

A traditional garden centre, also owned by David Penny, which opened in 1992. They can design, plant or construct gardens for you, offering the complete garden design. There is a pleasant, little gift shop, a second-hand book sales area and a children's play area. Part of the garden centre is leased to the Rutland Falconry and Owl Centre, owned by Chris Lawton. In total he has 46 birds and it is growing every year. Flying displays are carried out throughout the year so do call and view some of Europe's largest and most exciting birds of prey in flight. Chris will even put on a special display for a minimum of 10 people if they book in advance, any day of the week. There is an admission charge but it is well worth the money. Telephone 0378 152814.

Greetham

A very interesting village with three good pubs in a short space along the main road. Greetham possesses the remarkable home of William Halliday in Great Lane. This man was responsible for repairing several of Rutland's fine churches in the 19th century. He was a great hoarder of leftover stone and most of this material found its way to his workshop in Great Lane. It is impossible to miss his remarkable house, which is opposite the Viking Way footpath signpost to Exton in the village. If time allows do call at St Mary's Church, which was rebuilt in the late 19th century, or inspect Greetham Well which would not look out of place in the Peak District.

The Viking Way

The Viking Way is a long-distance footpath from the Humber Bridge through the Lincolnshire Wolds, and around the edge of the Fens, to the Vale of Belvoir and Rutland, finishing at Oakham. The total distance is 120 miles. Most the of the route follows public footpaths, bridleways and green lanes across the East Midlands countryside. Special yellow waymarker discs with a Viking helmet indicate the route direction throughout. For the Leicestershire section of 24 miles, a special leaflet has been prepared by Leicestershire County Council and is available from Tourist Information Centres.

Exton Park

Exton Park at one time extended to 607 hectares (1500 acres) of deer park. It is the home of the Earl of Gainsborough but the estate is now run by his son, Viscount Campden. The ruins of the original Exton Hall are nearby. The estate is private and walkers must keep to the well-signposted routes that pass through the park. The most interesting feature of the park is Fort Henry. This pretty, Gothic summerhouse was built on Fort Henry Lake at the end of the 18th century.

The Route

Walk along the track from the car park to Oakham Road then turn left into Greetham village. Go past The Plough public house, ignoring the Viking Way public footpath signpost, then past the Black Horse Inn as far as Wheatsheaf Lane, just before The Wheatsheaf.

Turn right down the lane to a public footpath signpost where you turn left on to a grassy path. At a yellow-topped waymarker post continue along the field edge, keeping close to a stream. Walk along the next field perimeter path to reach a plank across a stream. Cross and, now with the stream on your opposite side, continue as before to come to a stile.

A field path strikes uphill to the next stile where a field perimeter path runs alongside a mature hedge. Follow this field around to locate a stile well-hidden in the hedge. Climb out on to Greetham Valley Golf Course and turn left along the side of the fairway. An obvious path allows you to find a large gap in the hedge, which you must turn through. Continue ahead along the track, following it to the right to reach the new brick-built club house. Pass to the left of the building, following the waymarker arrows to the car park where a yellow-topped waymarker post is positioned.

Go downhill as indicated, then turn left along a tarmac track overlooking the lakes of the golf course. Bear right on to an access drive to Quinton Lodge then filter left on to a grassy bank. A undefined field path brings you to a stile on the right-hand side of the field. Join the pleasant path that now follows alongside North Brook. Climb a stile by a broken gate then continue along the grassy path to the next stile.

The next section may be difficult in summer as the path goes through a very overgrown, small wood which is full of nettles. A number of steps lead you up on to a woodland track and a public

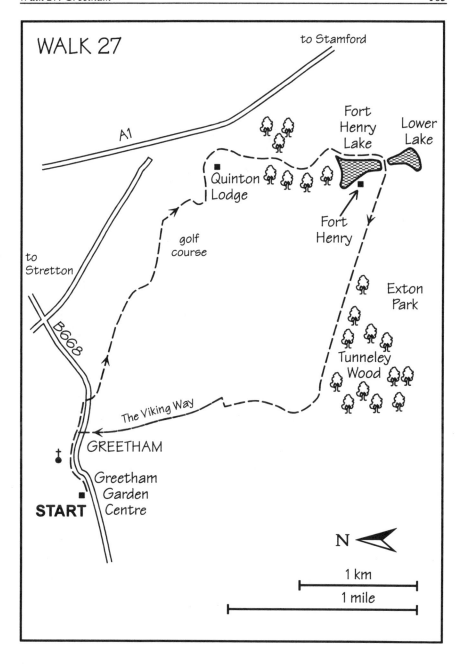

WALK 27

to Stamford

A1

to Stretton

B668

Fort
Henry
Lake

Lower
Lake

Quinton
Lodge

golf
course

Fort
Henry

Exton
Park

Tunneley
Wood

The Viking Way

GREETHAM

Greetham
Garden
Centre

START

N

1 km

1 mile

footpath signpost. Turn right along the woodland path for 50 metres before turning left down a flight of steps to rejoin the grassy footpath. The path follows alongside North Brook again with Osprey Wood further over to the right. A pretty tree-lined area is then passed through. Around the corner is the magnificent sight of Fort Henry Lake with the summerhouse standing across the water.

Do spend time here drinking in the scene before continuing uphill on to a grassy path that overlooks the water. At a public bridleway signpost, turn right and walk along the estate road in Exton Park to a waymarker post. Continue uphill on the estate road for the next mile, ignoring a bridleway off to the left and walking alongside Tunneley Wood.

At a Viking Way signpost, leave the estate road, turning right towards Greetham (1½) miles. A track snakes ahead. At a stile by a Viking Way signpost, cross a field making for a small wood ahead. Cross the one-hand, wooden footbridge then pass through a small, wooden hand gate. Rejoin the track that skirts alongside the wood, ignoring a path off to the right. In a further 250 metres turn right on to a grassy track to locate a stile hidden in the hedge after 100 metres.

A field perimeter footpath now runs by a tall hedge before petering out. At the end of the field emerge on to a track to walk uphill, heading for the spire of Greetham church. Cross a cattle grid then in a further 300 metres climb a wooden stile by a caravan and camping site. The path ahead is enclosed by a fence and hedge and brings you to a high stile. The thin path is now enclosed by overhanging trees. The road in Greetham village will be reached in a further 200 metres. Turn left and walk along the road through Greetham village to the tea room at Greetham Garden Centre.

Walk 28. Redmile

Route: Peacock Farm – Redmile Mill Bridge – Grantham Canal – Redmile – Barkestone-le-Vale – Grantham Canal – Peacock Farm Tea Room.

Start: Peacock Farm and Feathers Restaurant, Redmile. GR 791369

Distance: 3½ miles

Maps: OS Landranger 129 Nottingham and Loughborough area and OS Pathfinder 834 Radcliffe on Trent and Keyham.

Terrain: Flat walking through the beautiful Vale of Belvoir, along well-used footpaths. Interesting towpath walk by the Grantham Canal (disused).

Public Transport: Melton Mowbray – Stathern – Bottesford service calls at Redmile quite frequently, operated by Barton Buses. (Vale Runner number 2.) No Sunday service.

By Car: Redmile, two miles south-east of Whatton, is best approached from the A52 Bingham to Grantham road. It can also be reached by using minor roads from the A606 Melton Mowbray to Nottingham road, initially signposted to Belvoir Castle and then Plungar.

The Tea Shop

The tea shop at Peacock Farm is rather unusual as there is no one designated area where teas are served. Depending on the time of day, home-made cakes and cream teas are available in the Feathers Restaurant, the Tapas Bar or outside in the garden. For walkers and cyclists in a hurry a mug of tea and a crumpet can be purchased, while afternoon tea will more than likely mean that you will spend a cosy time meeting friends. Jacky Risenbuckler is responsible for the fine array of home-made cakes and delicious desserts, having taken out a franchise from owner Nicky Reed in 1997.

At Peacock Farm and the Feathers Restaurant it is open house every day of the week and a new style of eating is on offer. The Tapas Bar is available all day, if something more substantial is required choose from appetisers, small and large portions from a variety of English and continental regional dishes, breakfasts, and a farmhouse menu. À la carte and vegetarian menus and theme evenings make this a wonderful venue for eating. You can even stay in the guest house if you are so inclined, giving perhaps a weekend of great walking in the Vale of Belvoir.

Opening Hours: All day, Monday to Saturday. Closed Sundays in the winter. Telephone 01949 842475

Peacock Farm

The Peacock Farm, the guest house and The Feathers Restaurant is situated half a mile out of the village of Redmile and set in glorious Vale of Belvoir countryside. The farmhouse was originally an inn where canal bargees would stop to refresh themselves and their horses. The 'peacock' refers both to the family crest of the dukes of Rutland, owners of the farm until 1936, and also to the elderly topiary yew on the front lawn. In 1963 the old cow byre was converted into a bungalow and in 1973 Peacock Farm became a guest house again. In 1983 a small restaurant was opened in the old corn barn, thus reviving a licence that had lapsed in the last century.

Redmile

The village derives its name from the soil which has a high ironstone content, giving a reddish mould appearance. Redmile was popular with Central TV in the 1980s and early 1990s, when quality dramas such as Boon and Auf Wiedersehen Pet were set in this part of the Vale of Belvoir. In fact, Ye Olde Windmill Inn at Redmile doubled as The Barleymow in the latter series. St Peter's Church has a crooked spire and a beautiful interior, and is well worth a visit.

Grantham Canal

Although the canal is disused, it is a haven for wildlife and extremely popular with naturalists. Built in 1793, the canal stretches for a distance of 33 miles from Nottingham to Grantham. The most picturesque part of the old canal passes through the Vale of Belvoir. It is a mecca for wildfowl so look out for families of swans basking on the grassy towpath. It is hoped that one day the Grantham Canal Restoration Society will restore the canal back to its former glory and open it again as a navigable route.

The Route

Peacock Farm lies at the junction of roads to Barkestone-le-Vale and Redmile. Cross to Barkestone Lane opposite and in 100 metres the disused Grantham Canal will be reached at the former Redmile Mill Bridge. Turn left on to the grassy towpath, which feels like a deep-pile carpet beneath your feet, and walk ahead. You are immediately greeted with a superb view of the magnificent Vale of Belvoir. Upon reaching bridge number 54, Redmile Town Bridge, leave the canal, turning left on to Main Street. Pass the Peacock Inn – the car park of the pub was the former canal wharf in Redmile.

Opposite St Peter's Church turn right on to Church Lane and follow the road, passing Valley Farm. At a public footpath and byway signpost, turn right, crossing a cattle grid to an access road that leads to the sewage works. Immediately bear right across a field to a yellow-topped waymarker post and stile. Go over the next field to an old, metal gate, where a stream is crossed. A grassy, diagonal field footpath brings you to the next yellow-topped waymarker post and stile. Barkestone-le-Vale, with the tall spire of the church protruding into the skyline, can be seen, while across to the left is the fairytale-like Belvoir Castle. An obvious field path continues in the same manner as before to a stile. Cross several more fields to reach a public footpath signpost in the village of Barkestone-le-Vale.

Turn left along Fish Pond Lane then left again on to Town End. Turn right on to Chapel Street, then follow the road to the road junction by the old school. Cross Plungar Lane to the green then continue

A rural scene at Barkestone-le-Vale

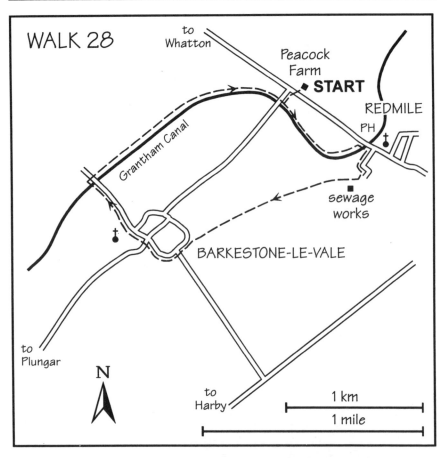

along Jericho Lane, passing the entrance to the church. Ignore the public footpath signpost on the left to Granby, continuing along the lane with superb views of the Vale of Belvoir into Nottinghamshire.

Upon reaching the bridge over the disused Grantham Canal, turn left down to the grassy towpath then go beneath bridge number 51 to rejoin the alluring waterside path again. Little direction is now needed as you make your way along the towpath, but do keep a sharp eye out for the many different species of wildfowl that frequent the canal. After a quarter of a mile of very pleasant walking, the white gates of Redmile Mill Bridge will be reached.

Leave the canal, turn left again on to Barkestone Lane and follow the road back to Peacock Farm and the conclusion of a very satisfying walk.

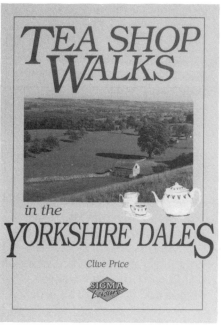

More Tea Shop Walks!

Enjoy even more easy walks with the reward of a typical English afternoon tea! *Each book is £6.95.* Areas include:

Cheshire - our local area, renowned for dairy products

The Chilterns - the first tea shop book we published!

The Cotswolds – more tea shops per square mile than anywhere else in the UK!

Hampshire – coastal and countryside walks

The Lake District (plus our brand-new **'More Tea Shop Walks in the Lake District'** for 1998!)

Lancashire – steeped in history, with a superb variety of walks and teashops in unusual locations!

North Devon – visit the land of world-famous coastal scenery and traditional farmhouse teas

The Peak District – rugged hills, gentle valleys and welcoming teashops

Shropshire – this rural county has so much to offer the discerning walker and teashop connoisseur

South Devon - including Dartmoor, the perfect companion to our North Devon title

Staffordshire – undiscovered by many walkers but a delightful walking and tea shop county!

Surrey & Sussex – a book of contrasts covering the very best of two counties

Warwickshire – Stratford is featured, plus many more locations off the tourist track

The Yorkshire Dales – a walker's paradise with traditional teashops

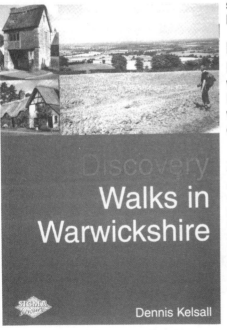

Notes

We update our books regularly. Please use this page to record any changes (e.g. in opening hours or possible footpath diversions) and send a copy to Sigma Press. Our fax number is 01625-536800; our postal address is on the back cover.